MOUNTAIN
MODERN

MOUNTAIN MODERN

Contemporary Homes in High Places

Dominic Bradbury ✳ Photographs by Richard Powers

CONTENTS

INTRODUCTION

Building on top of the world

'The mountains,' said John Ruskin, 'are the beginning and end of all natural scenery.' Certainly, there is no kind of landscape more mesmerizing nor more daunting than the great mountain ranges. They have the ability to both seduce us and terrify, they inspire both awe and affection. Only the sea, perhaps, has the natural power to compete with the majestic and ungovernable character of the mountains.

Just as we have been constantly seduced by the idea of making a home by the coast, so the mountains also have an intrinsic allure. They represent an extreme way of living, but one that many of us find almost irresistible. It is perhaps, above all, a love of extremes that draws us to the mountains in the first place.

For climbers, skiers and hikers, the hills and mountains represent an extreme physical challenge, as well as a source of deep pleasure and reward. For artists and photographers – and one thinks especially of Ansel Adams, the great American photographer and environmentalist – the rugged mountain landscape represents a source of great visual drama and depth. The view from the mountains gives us another kind of perspective upon the world – a bird's-eye view looking downwards, or a god-like, all-encompassing panorama.

Over the centuries, the mountains have also been recognized as a source of health and vitality. As well as the physical exertions of winter sports, the hills and mountains are an essential source of clean air and mineral water. Athletes might prefer high-altitude training to improve their stamina and fitness; others indulge themselves in mountain spas and health resorts. Just as the Victorians might have gone to the coast for a rest cure, they might also have taken themselves off to the mountains. The notion of a mountain resort grew in stature in the nineteenth century, and then really came into its own in the post-war period as skiing became an increasingly important recreational pursuit.

For architects, too, as well as many of their clients, the mountain landscape offers a powerful context in which to design and build. Creating and constructing a home in such an unforgiving environment can be deeply challenging on a technical level, with the need for a high-performance building that can cope with extremes of temperature and climate. But the opportunity to create a window upon such powerful countryside, to find a way of both framing the vista and connecting with it, has a tangible allure. Building in such a context demands a certain sensitivity to nature itself, but within this

An artwork by Peter Liversidge graces the wooded grounds of Cloudline (pp. 200–7), a house designed by architect Toshiko Mori, situated in Columbia County, New York.

epic landscape a building, when well conceived and crafted, can assume a particular resonance as a sculptural object placed in isolation upon this broad, open natural backdrop. Layers of snow at wintertime lend a new emphasis upon the purity of form and the clarity of the architect's composition.

While acknowledging the physical and logistical demands of building in such an environment, contemporary architects also have a rich heritage of alpine architecture to draw from as a source of inspiration and reference. Much of it is highly contextual and vernacular, with mountain communities drawing upon easily accessible local materials – particularly timber and stone – to create farm buildings, barns and homes that might be able to offer shelter and retreat from the often unforgiving climate of the hills and peaks.

Indeed, the mountains seem to have given rise to their own kind of house – the chalet, which can be seen with variations not just in the European Alps but also in other parts of the world. The timber chalet remains an alluring typology for architects and home owners today, particularly when given contemporary relevance and reinterpreted for modern living. The cabin, too, has a similar draw based upon its simplicity, its modesty, lack of pretension and the natural, easy way that cabins tend to sit within the landscape. Cabins and chalets have gained a new audience among those seeking a way of building sustainably and subtly, as well as contextually. The design of larger contemporary villas, too, has been increasingly influenced by the green agenda and the need for buildings that respect the landscape in which they sit, rather than simply seeking to impose themselves upon it.

In the twentieth century, many key architects have been drawn to mountain contexts and have sought to bring something new to the form and aesthetic of the mountain home. Carlo Mollino designed a series of modernist-influenced chalets in the Italian Alps in the mid-century period, while Charlotte Perriand worked on a number of residences and apartment buildings at Les Arcs in the French Alps, and had a lifelong love of skiing and hiking. Marcel Breuer helped to create the French ski resort of Flaine in the Haute Savoie, designing a series of buildings in the town. In more recent years, Swiss architect Peter Zumthor has established himself as one of the key voices of the alpine region with projects that include his much-lauded hotel spa in Vals.

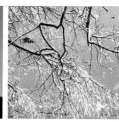

> 'I found a high point of land where I could stand and feel the great reaches of the Earth ... I wanted the shape of it to sing an unencumbered song.'
> CHARLES DEATON

In America, a number of pioneering twentieth-century architects created landmark houses within a mountain context. They include Albert Frey, who designed a house for himself up in the mountains overlooking Palm Springs, California. John Lautner also designed a landmark house up in the hills above the same city: the mesmerizing Elrod House, with its concrete, fan-shaped roof and mountainside swimming pool, where great slabs of rock push through into the interiors of the building itself. In Colorado, Charles Deaton created the Sculptured House on Genesee Mountain in 1965 – a futuristic space-age home, like a rounded shell facing out across the landscape from its prominent position on the hillside. 'I found a high point of land where I could stand and feel the great reaches of the Earth,' said Deaton. 'I wanted the shape of it to sing an unencumbered song.'

Designer Russel Wright, too, was seduced by the natural beauty of the hills and mountains, creating a home for himself – Manitoga – among the rugged landscape and former quarries of Dragon Rock near Garrison, New York, in the 1960s. The house he designed was highly sensitive to the countryside setting and his studio here featured an early example of a green planted roof.

These designers and architects were responding in many different ways to the romance contained within the idea of mountain living. The mountain house, more than almost any other kind of home, embraces the idea of escapism and the notion of crafting a retreat from the pressures and pace of the modern urban world. That is not to say that an alpine home cannot be contemporary or modern; the houses within this book suggest the depth and breadth to be found within the modern character and aesthetics of mountain residences. But the reasons that draw us to the mountains in the first place remain true and constant. The mountains will retain their hold upon us for a long time yet.

CABIN

CABIN

Introduction

When the American writer and philosopher Henry David Thoreau decided to build a cabin for himself at Walden Pond, it was part of a process of stepping back from the pressure of modern society and immersing himself in nature. 'I went to the woods because I wished to live deliberately,' he wrote, 'to front only the essential facts of life, and see if I could learn what it had to teach.'

Thoreau's modest, handmade cabin in woodland near Concord, Massachusetts, has become emblematic of the wish to step back, to draw breath and to retreat – if only temporarily – from the pace of everyday living. The cottage was just 14m² (150 sq ft) in size – a shingle-coated home, made of timber and plaster. But it had its own simple charm and barely intruded upon a landscape of particular beauty, celebrated in Thoreau's famous book *Walden; or, Life in the Woods*, first published in 1854.

Almost exactly a century later, one of the great prophets of modernist architecture also built himself a simple timber cabin, but this time overlooking the sea at Roquebrune-Cap-Martin on the French Côte d'Azur. Le Corbusier was, of course, one of the greatest thinkers and theorists of his age, and the author of books and buildings of great complexity and originality, yet he professed

to be at his most content when staying at his simple, wooden 'cabanon', designed on the corner of a table on 31 December 1951, in just forty-five minutes. The plans were definitive.

These two simple buildings, a hundred years apart, suggest a need for escape and a simpler way of living, surrounded by the beauty of the natural world. The materials and design were straightforward, the intentions honourable and the settings sublime. Today, when the pace of life and change seems faster than ever, the idea of our own cabin – away from everything – is more enticing than ever.

It is true, admittedly, that we seek a little more in the way of creative comfort from our cabins than Thoreau or even Le Corbusier might have anticipated. Yet the essential characteristics that might be said to define a cabin still ring true. It is a modest building, often but not always built in timber, which seeks to celebrate, respect and preserve the landscape in which it is set. The relationship between land and building is a crucial one, with the cabin little more than a gentle presence. It's a house that seeks to frame a particular perspective upon the countryside or mountainscape without intruding rudely upon it.

It's an architectural philosophy that sits perfectly with Australian architect Glenn Murcutt's maxim of 'touching the earth lightly'. Many

'I went to the woods because I wished to live deliberately ... to front only the essential facts of life, and see if I could learn what it had to teach.'

HENRY DAVID THOREAU

of his own buildings, including the Simpson-Lee House (pp. 74–81) in the Blue Mountains, New South Wales, are designed and built with the lightest of touches and with an emphasis upon sustainability, as well as the relationship between inside and outside space. But this is not to say that a cabin should have no ambition, original character or sense of beauty. Indeed, a modest building in a beautiful setting can represent a far greater achievement than a vast villa imposed upon a landscape with little thought for context or site. Even a small building – as Le Corbusier argued with his cabanon – can embody some big ideas.

Architect Alex Hurst's Holzkristal (pp. 32–41), designed for his mother on the outskirts of the small village of Lumbrein, Switzerland, is one building that contains many big ideas within a modest footprint. The name itself translates as the 'wooden crystal', suggestive of the sculpted quality of this cabin-like home, especially in the winter, when the black timber outline of the house stands out like a punctuation mark against the snow-covered pastures.

Other cabins on these pages have an equally innovative quality to their design, while retaining a modest scale and a love of the land. Architects Taalman Koch explored a fresh take on their prefabricated house-building system with an It Cabin (pp. 42–9), built in the mountains near Clear Lake, California, with not a neighbour in sight. London-based architectural firm DUST developed a low-slung triptych of pavilions in Arizona (pp. 68–73), looking out to the Catalina and Tucson mountains, made with rammed earth: a cabin with an organic warmth and texture, yet very different from the simple wooden structures built by Thoreau and Le Corbusier. They suggest, along with many other sensitively conceived new country houses and natural homes, the breadth and depth to be found within the familiar and much-loved cabin.

SIXTEEN DOORS HOUSE

Hillsdale, New York, USA
Incorporated

The house that architect Adam Rolston designed for himself in Upstate New York has not one front door, but sixteen. This is a seductive pavilion in the wooded hills, which opens up to the landscape and positively invites it inside through long sequences of glass doorways to front and back. And being a modest, single-storey building, this contemporary timber cabin celebrates this landscape, rather than seeking to dominate it.

'I tried plans with an extra bay to make eighteen doors, which felt too much, and fourteen doors felt too little,' says Rolston, a partner at New York-based practice Incorporated, who designed the house for himself and partner Martin McElhiney, a research psychologist. 'It was about finding a perfect, minimum scale that we were happy with. In a way, the whole of the house becomes our front door, and the fact that we have no distinct entrance takes away some of the formality about the way that the house works.'

A few hours' drive north up the Taconic State Parkway, the rural site is bordered by the Berkshire mountains to the east and the Catskills to the west. The design of the house – which mixes Scandinavian and Japanese influences with the simplicity of form found in the local cow barns – makes the very best of its hillside location, while the trees surrounding the building were carefully preserved during construction and now act as a natural sunscreen.

'We were looking for a piece of land for quite a while,' Rolston says. 'There was very little for sale at the time, but then we came across this hillside plot in the Hudson Valley, not far from the town of Hillsdale. In a way, the form of the house was already designed in my head, as I'd been playing with ideas for years before finding the land to build it on. It was a dream house.'

The notion of sophisticated informality carries through the interiors of the house, which are largely open plan. Seating, dining and kitchen areas are contained in one generous space in the centre of the building, while bedrooms and bathrooms are positioned at opposite ends. Usually the bedrooms remain partially open to the rest of the house, enhancing the feeling of single-space living, unless the twin pocket doors are pulled shut for privacy.

The house is set within a clearing upon a wooded hillside, with a strong sense of connection to the natural beauty that surrounds it. An outdoor fire pit offers an alluring focal point for evening relaxation.

Floors in American black walnut tie the house together, while furnishings mix pieces designed by the couple with junk-shop treasures, mid-century gems and an occasional piece of salvage found in a Manhattan skip. Blend these together with a few choice pieces of self-made art, and the effect is warm, layered and textured.

'There were two big splurges in the house, one of which was the walnut for the custom kitchen cabinetry and the floors,' says Rolston. 'The other big cost was the doors, which were actually made by a Canadian company from sustainable timber. Part of the reason for the scale of the house came down to cost and not wanting any excess of any kind. But at the same time, the building is also mathematically pure. It came down to thinking about how little we could have and still feel comfortable.'

Eco-friendly measures, apart from the timber construction and sensitivity to the landscape, include high-spec insulation and a wood-burning stove from Denmark. 'Everyone talks about the cost of sustainable design, and high-tech solutions can be quite expensive,' Rolston continues. 'But there are so many simple things you can do that many Americans seem to have forgotten about, things to do with orientation for maximizing light and how you deal with the landscape. Here, when the trees are bare in winter, the sun helps heat the house up beautifully, but then in summer, when the leaves are out, the shade of the trees helps keep us cool. It's a natural brise soleil and it doesn't cost a fortune.'

For the couple, who also have a modest apartment in the city, one of the great pleasures of the house, apart from regularly escaping urban life, is the fact that they now have the space to invite friends for the weekend and entertain.

'It's a great house for entertaining,' Rolston says. 'In the winter, we might just have smaller dinners or not entertain so much, but in the summer we open the house right up. We spend a lot of time on the deck, and when we have parties people flow back and forth between the fire pit at the back and the view to the front. Entertaining at home is not something we could really do in the city, so it's really fun to have a place that can be part of our social world.'

SITE PLAN

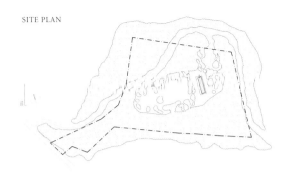

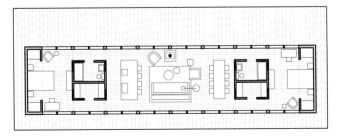

FLOOR PLAN

Above The deck provides a natural extension to the internal living space and is furnished as an outdoor room with a bespoke table and benches designed by the couple.

Opposite The house is coated in pine boards, stained black, and the deck is made with the same timber.

Above The copper console table behind the sofa was designed by Martin McElhiney.

Left The main living area is an open-plan space at the centre of the building. The kitchen is a bespoke design in American black walnut, while the sofa is a reupholstered 1970s piece.

Above Vintage finds and unusual treasures
in the master bedroom and the main living
area convey the house's sense of character.

Opposite The dining table is a custom
design by the couple; the large photograph
on the wall is also by Rolston.

FERIENHAUS GIRARDI

Bregenz, Austria
Philip Lutz Architektur

The mountain of Pfänder, with its cable-car station and transmission mast, towers over the Austrian border city of Bregenz. From the summit, you can see right across to Germany and Switzerland, and Lake Constance is spread out like a glimmering platter before you. Here, within a small hamlet of houses gathered on the mountain top, interior designer Christine Girardi commissioned a unique and escapist haven for herself and her family.

As residents of Bregenz, Girardi and her family knew the mountain well and often hiked up at weekends, returning by cable car. They found a small one-room cabin for sale and asked local architect Philip Lutz to replace it with a new, contemporary home for use at weekends and during the holidays. To preserve the existing trees on two sides, Lutz pushed the new house into the hillside, resulting in an irregular, sculptural shape. The finished building is a wooden jewel box – clad in black-stained pine shingles – which makes the most of the dramatic views of the lake in one direction and the mountains in the other.

'In addition to the two large trees, which we wanted to keep, the site is steep and quite public, and therefore complex,' says the architect. 'So we decided to follow the slope with the house itself. The main entrance is at mid-level, so that it can still be used when there is deep snow. The year we built the house, we couldn't even start work until May because of all the snow. You have snow risk right through from October to May, because Pfänder is 1,060m [3,478 ft] high.'

The house is steel-framed, but the predominant material inside and out is pine. Windows frame views of the lake and the mountain landscape, with a number of large sliding windows in key parts of the house that fully retract to become open balconies with integrated guard rails. There is also a balconied terrace at the top of the building, facing towards the mountains and the Swiss border. Importantly, the client wanted a home that was open and light. 'We wanted a very open house without having lots of separate, tiny, single rooms,' says Girardi, who shares the house with her husband and two teenage children. 'We didn't want a guest room, or even a children's room.'

The house is covered in pine shingles, stained black, in keeping with the neighbouring houses. The two linden trees on the site were preserved, partly dictating the unusual and sculptural shape of the building.

'The clients wanted a cocoon, or a squirrel's nest,' adds Lutz, who has known the family for many years. 'They explained that they wouldn't be here every single day, and so they didn't want to separate themselves from each other or the children. They want to see each other, to cook and talk. Part of the time they are just here as a couple, so they wanted a nest that they could share.'

The result was a house with very few solid doors or divisions. Instead, a series of split levels, or half-levels, step upwards and downwards from the entrance hallway. Arriving at mid-level, visitors find themselves moving straight into the kitchen, which is graced by a large window that frames an arresting view of the lake. Upstairs is a dining area and a children's den, which doubles as a media room, with access to the terrace alongside. Downstairs is the main sitting room with a fireplace and built-in sofa; the broad timber steps here have space enough for additional auditorium-style seating. The master suite is towards the lower section of the house and features a number of bespoke, built-in elements, including the bed and an integrated bath. A garage, store and utility room is located in the lowermost portion of the building.

Pine ceilings, walls and floors give a cohesive, cabin-like atmosphere to the house, but this is offset by a number of graphic black elements, mostly in steel. These include the fireplace, the framework and banisters for the stairs and, in places, exposed steel beams. The kitchen island is another black, sculpted element, with a custom lighting fixture above, also in welded steel; the kitchen units are in maple. With high standards of insulation and a degree of solar gain, the house warms up quickly and is relatively cheap to heat and maintain. The house is used all year round, but particularly in the winter when the cable-car route makes the house easily accessible and the family can sometimes ski from the house.

'The best time of day at the house is the early morning and sunset, when it is very peaceful,' says Girardi. 'Two years after we finished the house, our neighbour decided to cut down three huge trees that blocked our view of the lake. We never had the view before, but now we have it all the time. It's one of the best things about being at the house.'

GROUND FLOOR

FIRST FLOOR

Above Graphic black elements, including the fireplace, staircase and exposed steel beams, punctuate the cosy wood interior.

Opposite The ceilings, walls and floors are all in pine, creating a cohesive, cocooning feeling to the house.

Above The master suite is positioned on the lowermost level of the house, yet given the prominent nature of the site, the room still enjoys a strong vista.

Opposite The bespoke bed was designed by Christine Girardi; the space also features an integrated bath.

Above The steps down to the sitting room also serve as additional seating; the kitchen beyond is a custom design.

Opposite The house features many specially designed elements, including the steel fireplace and the L-shaped sofa in the sitting room.

Above A television den at the top of the house doubles as a second bedroom for the children.

Opposite Large picture windows, such as the dramatic opening in the dining room, make the most of the views of the mountain scenery and Lake Constance.

HOLZKRISTAL

Lumbrein, Switzerland
Hurst Song Architekten

When the snow falls in the mountains, Christina Hurst's home becomes a clear, black punctuation mark on a crisp, white sheet of paper. With its timber coat painted with a dark layer of pitch, this house on the edge of the village of Lumbrein has echoes of the hay barns that dot the mountainsides of the area. But Christina's house is also markedly contemporary, with an irregular, twisted copper roof and large panes of glass interrupting the timber façade. When she first saw a model of her house, she thought it looked like a wooden crystal, hence the name of the building, 'Holzkristal'.

It is an extraordinary location to build a home, with mesmerizing views along the valley, which points in the direction of the Italian border. The next valley over holds Vals, with its famous thermal spa; Lumbrein is better known for its artisanal cheeses, and is an escapist haven with few tourists to unsettle the peace. In the summer months, Hurst's home sits among green pastures, while in the winter the snow fields lap at the door and the house becomes a belvedere for appreciating the epic wonderland outside.

Christina already knew the area, as her mother once had an apartment nearby. Having lived in England before settling in Zurich, she decided that she missed the mountain air and began thinking about buying a property near Lumbrein. But with her son Alex an architect with his own practice, mother and son began to talk about building a house instead. A site was bought just outside the village, alongside a freshly cut road with a number of plots on it that had been set aside for building. Alex began working on a design that would push the house gently into the hillside, with garaging on the basement level and three floors of living space above. His mother had no strong views on what the house should look like, only that it should be flexible and adaptable.

The house's crystalline shape was partly influenced by the local building codes, which require the slope of a roof to be parallel to the slope of the mountain. But as the house sits on a corner site, Alex and his team came up with the idea of twisting the copper roof. Another planning code requires a large overhang for the roof over the body of the house, usually 1.4m (5 ft). After

The house, with its dark coat of timber, stands out against a blanket of snow in winter; the form of the house carries echoes of wooden agricultural buildings common to the region.

some constructive discussion with the architect about his plans, the local planning authorities allowed the overhang to be reduced down to just 4cm (1½ in.), thus preserving the sculptural outline of the building, which helps to define its unique character.

Inside, a large bunk room with three fold-down double beds sits to one side of the entrance hallway on the ground floor. The middle level holds the main living spaces, where Christina spends most of her time, with a large living room on one side of the central staircase and the combined kitchen and dining room to the other. A large picture window looking up the valley dominates the living room, which also has its own wood-burning stove, while the kitchen leads out onto a modest veranda slotted into the rear outline of the house. Upstairs, tucked within the pitch of the roof, are two other bedrooms with en suites.

'The house can be used in many different ways,' says Alex. 'When all the grandchildren are here, each bedroom can be used as a family suite, and the bunk room can sleep six. Rather than lots of small rooms, we decided to have three large bedrooms, which are each big enough to function as a retreat, like a comfortable hotel room.'

Alex pared down the materials used to a limited palette: concrete to strengthen the base and lower floors of the house; and pine used throughout, interspersed with the big windows. Architect and client worked closely with a local carpenter and builder, who also made the bespoke kitchen and the maple-topped dining table. Vintage pieces of furniture and flea-market finds are mixed with mid-century classics by Le Corbusier, Warren Platner, Harry Bertoia and Max Bill. The house is also built to a Passivhaus standard, with excellent insulation and a ground-source heat pump for the underfloor heating, along with a heat-recovery system to ensure that no energy is wasted in winter. The ethos of sustainability is echoed in the house's modest positioning within its site, with no formal gardens or landscaping.

'We tried to reduce the outside elements,' says Alex. 'There are just two seating areas outside and the house sits directly in the pasture. The cows come right up to the building, and that's how the grass gets trimmed.'

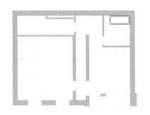

ENTRY LEVEL

GROUND FLOOR

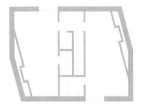

TOP FLOOR

Above The interiors were designed for flexibility, offering a comfortable experience for one but also adapting with ease to visiting family and guests, who can make use of the folding beds in the entry-level guest room.

Opposite The sculptural, crystalline form of the house was, in part, a response to the topography of the sloping site.

A large picture window in the sitting room offers a panoramic view of the village and neighbouring farms. The coffee table is a vintage Warren Platner design, while the armchair is an antiques-shop find.

Above The dining room at mid-level looks out over the snow-coated pasture to the rear of the building. The paintings in the sitting room are by Kieran Hurst, the owner's grandson.

Opposite The dining table is a bespoke design by the architect, while the chairs are vintage Horgenglarus designs.

Above The portrait of a Swiss farmer used
to belong to Christina Hurst's grandparents
and hung in a restaurant they once owned.

Opposite Two generously proportioned
double bedrooms sit at the top of the
house; the chair and ottoman in the
corner are by Harry Bertoia for Knoll.

IT CABIN

Clear Lake, California, USA
Taalman Koch Architecture

The journey to Terry Ohm's cabin is something of a pilgrimage. From San Francisco, the drive is around three hours, and from the highway, visitors move onto a mountain road and finally a dirt track, 29km (18 miles long), which winds its way upwards into the Mayacamas mountains. Ohm's nearest neighbour is 4km (2.5 miles) away, and there are no utilities or services, but the reward is a location of outstanding natural beauty, removed from everything, with the house sitting alone in splendid isolation.

'I'm at the peak of the Mayacamas, so I can see Clear Lake in the distance,' says Ohm, 'and I'm a few miles from the border of the Mendocino National Forest. The land here is maintained by the state as a natural environment, so it's very much about living in nature.'

While living in San Francisco, Ohm spent a couple of years hunting for the right spot to build his own country cabin, until at last a client recommended a spot in the Mayacamas mountains. But while the site might be sublime, the remote location threw up obvious challenges when it came to building a home here. The house not only had to be off-grid, but also relatively easy to assemble.

Ohm began researching prefabricated systems, and soon came across Linda Taalman and Alan Koch's It House, which they had begun developing in 2005. They have now completed around a dozen buildings, including their own off-grid house in the Joshua Tree National Park, in southeastern California. From the beginning, the It House was designed with sustainability in mind, using modular, factory-made components to help reduce time on site and transport and energy costs. The system has a lightweight but durable aluminium frame and window surrounds, with floor-to-ceiling glass walls and sliding doors establishing a strong and constant relationship with the landscape. The interior layout and spec can be adapted to suit each client and specific site. Having visited the architects' own It House, Ohm was convinced that the system would be perfect for his mountain location.

'The transparency of the design really appealed to me,' he says. 'Thinking about where I wanted to live, being part of nature was really important to me.

The house sits within an isolated mountain setting without a neighbour in sight. The elevated position of the building provides dramatic views across the landscape.

And bringing anything up here does take extra effort, so having something that has a module capacity to it is advantageous.'

As a designer himself, used to complex projects, Ohm involved himself in the design and construction of the house, closely working with the architects. The standard design was modified in a number of ways to create a new prototype: the It Cabin. The house sits on a floating platform, 1.2m (4 ft) above the ground, creating a level, well-insulated base for both house and adjoining deck. Lifting the cabin also helps protect against termite and other pest damage. The floor plan, too, was adapted to Ohm's own specification.

'With the sloping mountain site, we always anticipated that the house would be on a platform,' says Taalman. 'Originally we thought of using wood and then changed to steel, and that is part of the identity of the It Cabin. Terry's house played a big part in the development of the whole It Cabin concept, and Terry himself brought many things to the table. It all went pretty smoothly.'

Building the house took around eighteen months, from initial excavation to completion. Ohm moved temporarily from San Francisco to the nearby community of Geyserville to supervise construction, including the elements needed to create a self-sufficient home. Solar panels provide electricity, and the house also has its own water well and septic field. Reclaimed Monterey cypress was used for flooring and cabinet work. The interiors are largely open plan, with the study and bedroom connecting with the sitting room, dining area and kitchen; only the bathroom is fully partitioned. The indoor–outdoor relationship is accentuated throughout, with three separate decks pointing to views in different directions.

'Each view has its own personality, and varies according to the time of day and the season,' Ohm says. 'In the summer I like to sit on the front steps in the morning and drink my tea – it's a way of getting myself inspired to start the day. Then at night I like to lie in bed and look out the window at the stars. I have many favourite spots.'

FLOOR PLAN

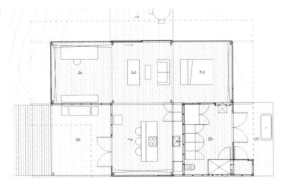

The house is raised off the ground to help protect it from termites, while additional insulation has been added to the base level of the building.

The main living spaces are contained within one open-plan space, with sliding glass doors to an adjoining terrace overlooking the trees and mountains.

The bathroom is the only fully partitioned space in the house. Even the sleeping area and study sit within the open-plan layout and enjoy the floor-to-ceiling windows.

TIMBER LAKE HOUSE

Sullivan, New York, USA
Rogers Marvel Architects + James Houston

For photographer James Houston, the experience of building this escapist retreat in the foothills of the Catskill mountains was one of pleasure and serendipity. The story of 'Ananda' – as Houston named the house, meaning 'bliss' – is only positive, with none of the occasional dramas and heartaches that seem to characterize many an ambitious design and build project. The end result is a building that is relaxed, comfortable and accomplished, but also opens itself up to the extraordinary landscape.

Houston, who grew up and worked in Australia before moving to the US, and his Scottish-born partner, restaurateur Brian McGrory, share an apartment in Manhattan's West Village. The pair had dreamt of a haven in the country for many years, nurturing an ambition to build a house of their own. 'When I first came up to the lakes, I thought it was so beautiful,' says Houston. 'The countryside is so amazing, and it has a feeling that you don't really get in Australia. It is a very special place.'

The couple's first stroke of luck was to find a local real-estate agent, who showed Houston to the site forty minutes after arriving in Madison County, and then pointed him in the direction of some talented local builders. The second was meeting architect Jonathan Marvel through a mutual friend at a house in Amagansett, Long Island, which he had designed. The plot of land sits at the edge of a lake, surrounded by woodland and hills, with no other houses in sight. 'The setting itself is spectacular,' Houston says. 'When you live in Manhattan with all the madness and energy of the city, you can't believe that in two hours you can drive to a place like this. It is so peaceful.'

Together with their client, Marvel and his colleague Shuji Suzumori were able to bring an international blend of influences to the design of the building. 'I'm from Puerto Rico,' he says, 'James is from Australia and Shuji is from Japan, and the three of us collaborated quite intensely on bringing our backgrounds to the project. There's an Australian kind of openness to the house and a brave-new-world quality. And because of the proximity to the water, it also feels a bit like a beach house. Shuji has an ability to synthesize nature and materials with

The house was carefully positioned for a mesmerizing view facing south over the lake, with pine trees all around.

real simplicity and elegance, and so there is an organic feel to the house with a lot of natural wood, stone, glass and steel.'

The internal layout of the house evolved from an idea about creating a series of more intimate spaces, such as the two guestrooms on the ground floor, which were almost like miniature cabins sitting beneath an overarching roof. Between them sits a generous, open-plan living space, anchored by a tower of stone that forms the fireplace.

'There's a sense of contrast between these different volumes,' observes Suzumori. 'I enjoy the quality of the spaces and the way that the living room flows into the dining room and then the kitchen. They are all part of a large space, but each one has a different character within this one big room.'

The living room soars upwards to the ceiling, 9m (30 ft) overhead, in this double-height section of the house, while the kitchen at the other end is more enclosed and sheltered, allowing space for a modest second storey with room for the master bedroom and bathroom, a mezzanine library and yoga studio. It is a more private sanctuary, away from guests, and a great vantage point for vistas of the lake and woodland.

Houston designed a number of pieces of furniture himself, including the day bed and dining table, and had them made in Indonesia. Other pieces of cabinetry were co-designed with the architects and made by the contractors. Some staples from Crate & Barrel went into the mix, blended with bespoke pieces and character finds from 'furniture hunter' Andrianna Shamaris in New York, including a sculpted wooden chair by the fireplace.

For Houston and McGrory, the house is a blend of Japanese-style minimalism and restraint that allows room for the eclectic mix of furniture and organic textures to breathe, along with an easygoing, Australian-style approach that emphasizes comfortable living and relaxed entertaining. There is also a focus on indoor–outdoor living, with the house opening itself up via its porches, decks and veranda to the landscape itself.

A strong relationship between inside and outside space is key to the design of the house, with fluid connections between the main living spaces on the ground floor and the deck alongside.

GROUND FLOOR

ELEVATION

The interior design combines Japanese-
inspired minimalism with an easy-going
Australian influence. The result is a house
that is comfortable and relaxed.

Above The kitchen was a design collaboration between architects and client.

Opposite The double-fronted fireplace and chimney breast provide a degree of separation between the seating and dining areas on the ground floor. The table is a bespoke design by Houston, and the chairs are from Room & Board.

Above The sculptural Agape bath in the
master bathroom is positioned to make
the most of the dramatic vista through
the picture windows.

Opposite The master bedroom features
a wood-burning stove and a bespoke bed
designed by Houston.

COLBOST HOUSE

Waternish, Isle of Skye, UK
Dualchas Architects

The landscape of the Isle of Skye, off Scotland's western coast, is full of fascination. This is where the sea meets the mountains in dramatic fashion, with the towering Cuillins dominating this, the largest of the islands of the Inner Hebrides. These mountains include twelve of Scotland's 'Munros', a term that refers only to peaks over 914m (3,000 ft) in height, and can be as challenging as they are beautiful. They also provide an extraordinary vantage point, looking out over the lochs and surroundings islands.

Dualchas Architects have designed around thirty contemporary houses on the island and have their main office here, as well as another in Glasgow. Their work appeals to an audience from much further afield on the strength of the team's sensitivity to the landscape, as well as the way their buildings splice vernacular sources of inspiration with a distinctive, contemporary aesthetic. When Anne and Matthew Williams decided to build their own home on Skye, the firm was a natural choice, and they took the project to principal Mary Arnold-Forster. 'We were clear from the outset that we wanted something different to the traditional, whitewashed Skye home,' says Anne. 'Mary showed us her own house, The Shed, and we liked the limited palette of materials used and its warmth, despite being open plan and with a large expanse of windows.'

The Williams family had known the island for many years and share a love of mountain landscapes. They found some land for sale to the northwest of the island, with views out across Loch Dunvegan to the Waternish peninsula and the islands of the Outer Hebrides, as well as the Cuillin peaks to the south. They commissioned a new-build home – initially for holiday use, but with the aim of treating it as a primary residence in the future – while Anne's sister built a house for herself and her family on the neighbouring plot.

'We wanted a home that would capture the light and the views of Skye, while at the same time being large enough to accommodate visiting friends and family in an open-plan, modern environment,' says Anne. 'We love the views from the site and the fact that our home is relatively unassuming, tucked away beneath an escarpment so that you hardly notice it from the road.'

The outline and appearance of this house of two distinct parts are reminiscent of a grouping of agricultural barns and sheds.

ELEVATION

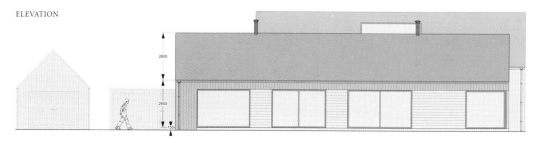

2600

2600

150

Architect and client shared an ambition for a design that would be both modest and in keeping with the context of the place. Arnold-Forster opted to divide the house into two distinct volumes to reduce its overall impact on the landscape. A double-height section to the front holds the main living spaces and makes the most of the views across the loch, while a second, two-storey section to the rear holds four bedrooms and a games room. Between the two sits the entrance hallway. Yet while the two interlinked structures lie parallel to one another, they are not fully aligned, rather like a pair of skis where one is slightly ahead of the other. Two separate, complementary structures to one side hold the garage and storage space, along with an air-source heat pump.

The outward appearance of the house, with its larch cladding stained an olive black, takes inspiration from traditional farm buildings of the region. 'We had no desire to build the big, white house, and wanted to reduce the bulk of the building into several more familiar forms,' says Arnold-Forster. 'There is a perfect black shed on the track going up to the site, which you could easily pass and overlook, and I really liked it. For me, the house is an abstracted shed, distilled down to the most important aspects of scale, form, site and proportion.'

The main living spaces are partially open plan, with the kitchen and dining area at the centre of the foremost structure and a long skylight bringing in extra sunlight from above. Two seating areas at either end are arranged around wood-burning stoves, while a large, sliding oak door can be used to isolate the pavilion from the hallway and sleeping quarters beyond. This tends to be pulled across in the evening to create a greater sense of intimacy. The master suite sits on the upper level of the house, where windows and skylights frame views of the escarpment and the rugged hills. The games room on the lower level can easily be converted into a fifth bedroom, if needed. This is, after all, a house with a welcome degree of flexibility to the ways in which it can be used, as well as a home of character and warmth.

The house is well positioned upon the hillside for views out across Loch Dunvegan and the rugged landscape of Skye. The smaller structures serve as a garage and storage for services and plant machinery.

SECTION

2300

Large floor-to-ceiling windows in the main living spaces at the front of the house offer a picturesque panorama over the loch and the distant hills of the Waternish peninsula.

Natural light is drawn into the bedrooms
and living spaces from a number of different
directions, adding to the rich quality of
the interior spaces. Window openings
include skylights, which feature in both
of the twin structures.

TUCSON MOUNTAIN RETREAT

Tucson, Arizona, USA
DUST

Few materials have as much history and heritage as rammed earth. It is one of the oldest and most traditional ways of building, yet still has the power to surprise and inspire. In recent years, rammed earth has been revisited and reassessed by contemporary architects in many countries, enticed by its environmental benefits, textural richness and adaptability. One of the most engaging of these new-generation rammed-earth homes sits within an extraordinary landscape where the mountains meet the Sonoran Desert in the southwestern United States.

Here, Cade Hayes and Jesús Robles of architectural practice DUST created a low-slung earthen cabin that sits naturally and modestly within the landscape, yet retains a sculptural, tectonic beauty and establishes a powerful relationship between indoor and outdoor living spaces. Both natives of the American southwest, Hayes and Robles have drawn upon the inspiration found within the epic, open landscape, as well as a love of craft and construction. Their work reinterprets the vernacular heritage of the region – including rammed-earth and adobe construction – in fresh, vivid contemporary buildings.

The design of the Tucson Mountain Retreat was both a response to its unique setting on the borders of the Saguaro National Park, with the Catalina and Tucson mountains rising up to the north and south, and a particular programme laid out by the owners. A couple with a grown-up daughter, the clients wanted a vacation home that might also serve as a retirement house in future years. They asked for a home that would include a soundproofed music and recording studio, bedrooms and a roof deck, with no wasted hallways between any of the spaces in the building.

'First and foremost was a love of the land,' says Hayes. 'The clients wanted something sensitive and harmonious. We tried to design a home that would fade into the background and let the desert and the mountains be a major aspect of the living experience.'

The resulting building, which DUST built as contractors as well as architects, is essentially a series of three interlinked pavilions. A series of eye-catching

The house sits within the foothills with views of the Catalina and Tucson mountains. The single-storey building, with its rammed-earth walls, is a modest and discreet presence in the landscape.

concrete steps – a playful but contemporary reimagining of stepping stones – leads to the main entrance and directly into the central pavilion, containing the living spaces. Kitchen, dining and seating areas can be found here within an open-plan layout, with sliding glass doors to either side leading out to a terrace at one side of the house and a generous veranda at the other. A hidden spiral stairway near the entrance rises up to the roof terrace, served by a dumbwaiter from the kitchen below.

A music and entertainment room sits within another pavilion at one end of the house, and two bedrooms – back to back – within a third structure at the other. Importantly, there are no internal doors between the pavilions, requiring residents and guests to step outside or onto the veranda to move between the three distinct zones. The bedroom pavilion also features a strong inside–outside relationship, with a long terrace alongside the two sleeping quarters. Many elements throughout the house, including the kitchen, staircase and much of the furniture, are custom designs.

Many common-sense design features shield the house from the desert heat: its position along an east–west axis to reduce solar gain; the projecting overhang of the roof, which shades the main living spaces from the high summer sun; and the use of natural cross-ventilation. The house is fed by water from a local well and includes rainwater-harvesting tanks, while solar electricity is an option for the future. The use of adobe also reinforces the green credentials of the house, given that it is an easily available, locally sourced and low-energy building material – as well as one with a rich depth of patina and tone.

'Adobe has ancient roots, and the bottom line is that it is beautiful in texture and emotion,' says Hayes. 'I fell in love with the material as a student, and it's easy to understand why when you experience it first hand. It has a tactile quality that really grabs at your heart. So when the clients expressed an interest in rammed earth, of course we jumped on board. It's of the place, and also grows from the place.'

FLOOR PLAN

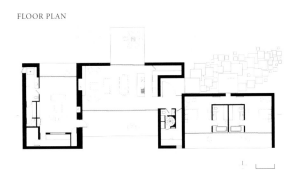

Generously scaled, sheltered verandas are a feature of the three pavilions that form the house. Occupants are obliged to step outside to move between them, enhancing the intense relationship with the surrounding landscape.

SIMPSON-LEE HOUSE

Mt Wilson, New South Wales, Australia
Glenn Murcutt

The community of Mt Wilson sits within the northern lands of the Blue Mountains in New South Wales. Here, at an elevation of just over 900m (3,000 ft), there can be snow in winter, while forest fires are a threat in the summer months. All around lies the epic beauty of the Blue Mountains National Park, which ranges over thousands of hectares. This was the natural context for a commission to build a new home that was to prove one of the most demanding and influential of architect Glenn Murcutt's career.

Murcutt has made an international impact as a sole practitioner, concentrating his work on houses and buildings that respect the Australian landscape and the natural environment, while 'touching the earth lightly'. His buildings are conceived with an emphasis on sustainability, but are also born out of the particular needs of his clients and the natural setting and conditions of a site. Geelum Simpson-Lee, a respected economist and academic, based at the University of Sydney, wrote to the architect asking him to design a house with 'a secular monastic quality' for himself and his wife Sheila.

'With every good building, as Mies van der Rohe said, there is a very good client, and that has to be acknowledged from the outset,' says Murcutt. 'It was an extraordinary process, and Geelum taught me many things. They were exceptional clients who made huge demands, on me personally and on my time and intellect. Geelum and I argued the whole way through about every design decision.'

The house sits on a sloping site in a forest of dark-trunked *Eucalyptus blaxlandii* and silvery *Eucalyptus oreades*. The programme involved two separate but complementary single-storey structures, one hosting a garage and pottery studio for Sheila's use, with the master pavilion containing a bedroom at either end, as well as the main, open-plan living spaces at the centre. Between the two pavilions sits a bridge-like walkway and a large collecting pond for harvested rainwater, which can be used for damping down and fire-fighting if needed. An angled mono-pitch roofline helps collect water for the pond, which has seen use during the dry months of summer.

The pavilion-like form of the single-storey house creates a contemporary cabin among the trees, which shelter and soften the building. The axial line of the house rests upon an aboriginal 'songline'.

The risk of fire partly dictated the choice of materials; blockwork for the base of the house and concrete floors, which formed a platform for a pavilion of steel and glass, with large windows to the front that slide away to establish a direct sense of connection with the forested landscape. But the architect found that his client's reaction to the initial designs was not positive.

'The drawings were ready to go to tender, and Geelum wrote me this terrible note,' says Murcutt. 'He said that he'd asked me to design a lightweight-looking house and not a battleship. I was very angry and wrote a letter of resignation and hung on to it for a week.'

The long dialogue between architect and client soon restarted, with Simpson-Lee suggesting more costly, bespoke components to help create a lighter exterior appearance to the house. It took nearly two years to get planning permission, given the unconventional style of the building, and the design-and-build process ultimately lasted six years in total.

'We became like father and son in the end, and I was the son,' says Murcutt. 'At the end of the job, Geelum put his arm through mine and said, "You know Glenn, there's one disappointment in this project: the process is over." I asked why we had to argue over every decision, and his reply was: "In economic theory you put up a proposition and argue it out. If it should fall, it falls. But if its stands up, then it has the potential to be a new theory. You put up a design, and I argued against it to see if you were serious about it." By the end of it, we had this amazing bond.'

When Geelum Simpson-Lee died some years ago, his wife Sheila continued to use the house, with the architect visiting often. When Sheila finally decided to sell, Murcutt himself bought the house, suggesting its importance within his own mind and within his architectural career. Perched upon such a vivid mountain setting, it is one of Murcutt's most fascinating houses – a cabin of steel and glass, floating among the eucalyptus trees.

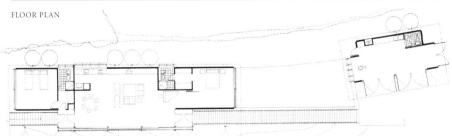

FLOOR PLAN

The main living spaces feature large sliding windows that retract to form an immediate connection with the surrounding woodland; the windows also help in providing cross-ventilation for cooling the building in summer.

The main body of the house is separated from its smaller twin, the pottery studio/garage, by a walkway and a water pool, which also serves as a reservoir for use in the event of a forest fire.

The house is positioned on a hillside, looking down the slope; from this vantage point, the tree canopy lends the house something of a treehouse character. Two bedrooms sit to either side of the open-plan living area.

CHALET

CHALET

Introduction

No other kind of building is as intimately associated with the mountains as the chalet. An endearing, romantic mythology has grown up around the chalet, and it retains a special hold upon the affections of many. Part of this is to do with the contextual character of traditional chalets and the way that they seek to align themselves with the landscape, becoming part of the natural beauty of the mountains, rather than seeking to impose something that might be alien or inappropriate on the countryside. The special sense of place and identity embodied by the chalet still has particular resonance.

Usually made with local timber or a combination of timber and stone, the alpine chalets of Switzerland, France, Italy, Austria and Germany featured steeply pitched roofs that protect against rain and allow heavy snow to fall away, rather than loading the building with more and more weight – a layer of snow can help to insulate a house in winter, yet too much would clearly be a danger. The pitched roofs generally project outwards to form a protective canopy around the building, sheltering windows and balconies, and the dry spaces around the house at ground level would often be stacked with firewood for the winter, with the extra layer of timber adding to the insulation.

Traditionally, some simple mountain chalets would only be used during the summer months by farmers and herdsmen grazing their livestock in the high pastures. Others would be lived in all year round, often with livestock in the lower level of the building during winter, which would help bring some extra warmth to the farming families living in the storeys above. Smaller, secondary wooden shelters, or *mazots*, were sometimes sited nearby, for storing possessions and food when the main house was left empty or as a kind of insurance against the very real risk of fire within the timber chalets, warmed by stoves and open fireplaces.

During the eighteenth and nineteenth centuries, vernacular alpine chalets began to attract the attention of travellers, writers and artists. John Ruskin wrote warmly of the simple beauty of the chalet in the 1830s. 'Its power was the power of association,' he suggested, and 'its beauty, that of fitness and humility'. He admired the way that these houses sat within the rugged countryside, pushed and tucked into hillsides to cope with the sloping ground and to provide an added degree of shelter. Their modesty was to be praised, with their evocative power suggesting a pastoral and peaceful way of living.

'Its power was the power of association
... its beauty, that of fitness and humility.'

JOHN RUSKIN

Ruskin emphasized the importance of context, warning against the temptation to simply export the chalet typology to other countries and climates with little thought of how appropriate, or inappropriate, they might be. But his message was not heeded and chalet architecture was exported around the world, adapted and updated to a whole variety of settings and situations, with more success in some cases than others.

In the twentieth century, the chalet became the lynchpin – or default architecture – of fast-growing mountain resorts in the European Alps, North America and other parts of the world. In many parts of Europe, building codes protected and preserved the chalet as part of the intrinsic identity of mountain communities. During the post-war years, as the ski industry grew, fed by new wealth and greater opportunities for leisure and winter sport, the pastoral connotations of the chalet blended with a romantic view of the mountain home as an escapist retreat, a place to recharge and rethink.

A number of influential modernist architects and designers shared this ongoing fascination with the chalet. Charlotte Perriand worked on a number of projects in the French ski resort of Méribel Les Allues in the 1940s, as the resort grew from almost nothing. These included the interiors of a chalet-style hotel, Le Doron, and her own modest chalet,

made of timber and stone; Perriand designed furniture for both projects, with her 'Tabouret Méribel' three-legged stool still in production today.

In Italy, Carlo Mollino was a polymath designer, architect, photographer and writer with a great love of skiing and the mountains. As well as writing and collaborating on books of ski techniques, Mollino designed a number of buildings in the Italian Alps in the 1940s and '50s. These included the Casa del Sole hotel in Cervinia, in the Valle d'Aosta region of northwest Italy, his own chalet in the Piedmontese town of Sauze d'Oulx, and the Furggen ski station. Like Perriand, Mollino was fascinated with ways in which he could bring a subtle sense of modernity to a very traditional type of building.

It's a welcome challenge that has been embraced by many contemporary architects, as the chalet continues to engage and inspire. From Switzerland to Austria to Canada, the new-generation chalets on these pages are very much in tune with the needs and amenities of twenty-first-century living, yet they retain an intrinsic respect for organic materials, familiar forms and, above all, the landscape itself, seen within chalet architecture, old and new.

MAISON GLISSADE

Blue Mountains, Ontario, Canada
Atelier Kastelic Buffey

There is just one artwork gracing the fresh, open-plan living spaces of Maison Glissade – a vast photograph of Sans Souci harbour, taken by artist Scott McFarland at Georgian Bay, Lake Huron, not far from the small town where Elisa Nuyten's country chalet is situated. For a passionate art collector like Nuyten, just having this one piece, which had to be craned into the building, shows considerable restraint. It came from a wish to let the house itself be the centrepiece, along with the views of the mountains that surround it.

'I felt as though I just wanted one important piece and that's about it,' says Nuyten, who serves on the board of Toronto's Power Plant Contemporary Art Gallery. 'I didn't want to clutter the house, because here it should be more about the simplicity of the design and the architecture. I needed this house to be different to the way that we live in Toronto.'

In the city, Nuyten has assembled a considerable art collection in the house that she shares with her husband, David Dime, and their three children. In town the look is sophisticated and urban, but for their Blue Mountains retreat, the atmosphere is more relaxed and informal. 'I didn't want the house to be bigger than our needs and as a family I wanted us to be close together,' she says. 'People say that the house has a very European or Nordic feeling, and I do like that sensibility a lot and I love Scandinavian furniture.'

The family owned a smaller house on the site, opposite a ski lift and gentle runs, but after three years they decided to build a contemporary chalet that was more tailored to their needs and tastes. One characteristic that they liked about the original building was that the main living spaces were on the top floor, with the bedrooms below – a pattern that was repeated in the new house by architects Kelly Buffey and Robert Kastelic of the Toronto-based practice Atelier Kastelic Buffey. As well as responding to the site and the views of the mountains, Buffey and Kastelic took inspiration from the simple forms of the local timber buildings. This fed into the pure, organic aesthetic of the cedar-clad house, where the timber is carried right over onto the roof, creating a cohesive, sculptural quality.

The house is a contemporary reinterpretation of the traditional chalet typology. The pure but engaging design drew inspiration from the mountain setting, as well as from the barns and other vernacular buildings of the region.

'We reduced down all the elements to make a very pure form, and then shifted the top volume so that it cantilevers over the lower volume,' says Buffey. 'The word "glissade" is a kind of forward movement used by climbers and skiers. The idea of the roof was to create the impression of a solid volume. If the roof was made of a different material, it would have undermined that.'

The house was designed to be durable, practical, flexible and low maintenance, so the floors in the entrance hallway are in poured concrete and feed straight into a combined boot and utility room, with bespoke cupboards for skis, helmets and outdoor clothes. Downstairs also holds two bathrooms and three bedrooms; at 223m² (2,400 sq ft), the chalet is reasonably modest in scale. But the house only reveals its true colours upstairs, with a generous open-plan layout creating the look of a country loft. Oak floors and banks of windows open out to a balcony at the front of the house and a deck and barbecue zone to the rear.

To avoid any solid partitions, the team created a fluid procession from the seating area to the central dining table to the kitchen, designed as a bespoke, freestanding piece of furniture, with an island topped in crisp Corian alongside, rather than as a solid partition. A punctured recess in the centre of the kitchen allows the eye to carry on through, while a small working study has been tucked away behind it. Client and architect collaborated on the choice of furniture, with a Linteloo sofa and Hans Wegner-designed 'Wishbone' chairs in orange for a splash of colour, standing out all the more against the clean backdrop of the white walls and timber floors. The large dining table, which seats twelve, is a bespoke piece by the architects, made of reclaimed hemlock, and adds a more rustic flavour.

'We all thought along the same lines,' says Nuyten. 'I like the fact that it all feels very fresh. The orange adds a very happy colour. And I love how the George Nelson lights turn the house into a lightbox at night. I like thinking of that lightbox idea before I close the curtains. It's like being inside a work of art.'

GROUND FLOOR

FIRST FLOOR

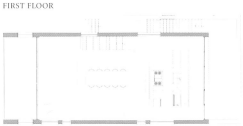

The dining table is a bespoke piece made from reclaimed hemlock, while the lights above are a classic George Nelson design. The 'Icicle' coffee tables are by Thomas Pedersen.

The 'Stingray' rocking chair is another piece
by Danish designer Thomas Pedersen. The
custom kitchen, with its Corian countertops,
was designed by the architects, and the stools
are by Clemens Weisshaar.

Above Bedrooms and bathrooms are on the
ground level, while the main living spaces
upstairs enjoy the best of the views.

Opposite The ski and boot room
is located next to the main entrance
on the ground floor.

STROLZ HOUSE

Lech, Austria
Dietrich Untertrifaller Architekten

The sheer drama and natural beauty of the Austrian mountain resort of Lech is startling and seductive. This is a place where the snow starts falling in November and will only clear in May or June. During the winter, the high altitude means that the snow can easily settle to a few metres in depth and the nighttime temperatures can fall to -30° C (-22° F). Lech is a great favourite for discerning skiers and an extraordinary place to raise a family, just as Marcell and Uli Strolz are doing.

With little traffic and a small, close-knit community, this is a place where parents can walk their children to school and where everyone learns to ski almost as soon as they can walk. Marcell Strolz grew up in the village and has seen it become a fashionable resort, but without succumbing to the temptations of mass development. It remains a relatively unspoilt village, so building in Lech can be something of a challenge, as no second homes are allowed within this small enclave up in the Arlberg mountains.

Contemporary architecture can be contentious here, and then there are factors to consider such as the extreme conditions and avalanche risk. The couple had to take all of this into account when they decided to build their own family home. Having project-managed the construction of the local biomass plant, one would expect Strolz to build a green building, and he has done just that and more, creating a striking, contemporary house on the edge of the village. Sitting right by the ski runs, with the mountains towering around them, it is a tantalizing spot for this timber-framed, larch-coated, eco-friendly home.

When the couple heard of a rare plot of land being sold by a local family, they grabbed their chance. Finding that the site was just on the border of the 'red zone', signalling avalanche danger, they factored this in to the sophisticated design of the house. As well as working as a project manager across a mix of different projects in the region (including the biomass plant, which supplies hot water for heating and domestic use for most of the village), Strolz also volunteers as part of the avalanche protection team for the village, so well understands the risks.

The building carries echoes of traditional timber barns and chalets nearby, yet the design is clearly contemporary, with large expanses of glazing looking out across the snow fields.

'We are right on the edge of the area where building would be allowed, and beyond us is a pasture where there will never be any other homes, because of the avalanche risk,' says Strolz. 'There is some steelwork, as well as the timber frame, to strengthen the house, and we also have a series of sliding wooden shutters to protect the building, plus specially strengthened glass.'

These wooden shutters can be closed off to seal the windows when an avalanche is imminent, or during the annual 'snow roll' from the nearby Omesberg mountain, which passes close by after a controlled explosion. There is also a retractable wooden wall, which disappears into the floor, to protect the open veranda at one end of the house. Even if the house were to be hit by an avalanche, Strolz is confident that both his family and the building would be fine, given all the protective measures.

The house was designed by Helmut Dietrich of Dietrich Untertrifaller Architects, and Strolz was closely involved throughout the process. 'I did all the preparation of the site, digging the foundations and pouring the concrete base of the house,' he says. 'The wooden frame was prefabricated by a local construction company, and went up in two days. I also did the dry walling, the floors, some of the electrics – it was quite a lot of work.'

The building is pushed gently into the hillside, with a large basement area holding a garage, boot room, storage areas and utility spaces, as well as the entrance hall. Flexibility was a key part of the design, with two separate apartments – one for rental and one for a nanny – integrated into the outline of the house, along with the family's own living space over two storeys. The main living space is open plan, leading out to the veranda, with the bedrooms and Strolz's study on the floor above.

The house is linked to the biomass plant, which feeds the underfloor heating, and Strolz also installed solar panels, which make the most of the winter sun. Even the layers of snow on the roof in winter add to the high levels of insulation that keep the house warm. The timber for the frame and larch cladding was sourced from sustainable forestry, making the house just about as green as one could hope for.

FLOOR PLANS

Sliding timber shutters can be pulled across the windows to help protect the house from the area's severe weather, or simply to provide internal shading on sunnier days.

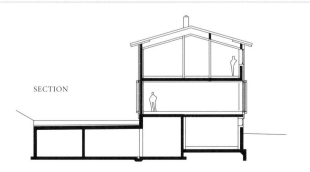

SECTION

Above and opposite The custom kitchen
looks out onto the neighbouring pastures,
which are buried in a deep layer of snow
during the winter.

Above right A separate apartment at
the top of the house looks out across
the rooftops of the nearby village.

Above Wood panelling and floors lend the interiors an organic quality; the red sofa in the sitting room is a 1960s piece that belonged to the owners' parents.

Opposite Views from the veranda suggest both the depth of the winter snow around the house and the drama of the mountains, which rise up on both sides of the valley.

HOUSE 0143

Sils, Switzerland
Küchel Architects

Architect Arnd Küchel certainly picked a powerful and resonant location –
in the Upper Engadine valley, not far from St Moritz – in which to build a
home for himself and his family. Here, the valley floor is broad and generous,
allowing views out across a collection of lakes, including Silvaplana and Lake
St Moritz, where the famous 'White Turf' horse races are held upon the frozen,
snow-covered surface in winter. The house benefits from the openness of the
lake plateau here, with the mountains towering over the valley to either side.

'It is a fantastic place,' says Küchel, who has lived in the area since he was
five years old, when his family made the move from Germany to Switzerland.
'If you move further along the valley, then it does become narrower, but at this
point it's wide and open. I have lived in this region for most of my life, apart
from the period when I was studying architecture. I think it makes you strong
when you can work in the area in which you grew up.'

Küchel bought a plot of land here, in the village of Sils, from his father-in-
law; his wife also grew up locally and her parents used to own a hotel nearby.
He took some inspiration from the vernacular barns and agricultural buildings
of the area when designing the house, which is clad in larch above a layer of
stone, with a generous entrance and hallway that looks big enough for a horse
and cart. But the house is also contemporary in character, with a crisp outline,
plenty of glazing and refined interiors in an organic, minimalist style.

'We really wanted to use local materials as much as we could,' Küchel says.
'The stone and wood are from the area and we used local craftsmen. It was
also important to blend the house with nature. If you see the house from the
outside, you would never expect the big, spacious volumes that we have inside.'

Küchel established his practice in St Moritz in 1991, shortly after finishing
his studies in Lausanne and Zurich. He has worked on a wide range of projects,
including the conversion of the 1928 Winter Olympics stadium into a home
for furniture retailer Rolf Sachs and a collaboration with Norman Foster on the
Chesa Futura apartment building in St Moritz, and eventually added another
office in Zurich.

The towering mountains of the Upper Engadine
valley form a powerful backdrop to the house,
with large picture windows that make the most
of the views.

In Sils, Küchel wanted to complete the construction of the house in just one seven-month stretch in the middle of the year, when the ground would be free of snow. He designed the building with a prefabricated larch frame, sitting on a concrete base, which went up in just eight days. High-spec insulation was used throughout, including sheep's wool, which also helps to control humidity levels in the house, while the outside layer uses larch cladding. Küchel took great care to use natural and local materials as much as possible, while creating a sustainable home, with a ground-source heat pump providing winter warmth.

Inside, the house ranges over three floors, with a basement level, alongside a subterranean garage and storage area, holding a large, multifunctional family room, as well as guest bedrooms and a wine cellar. The ground floor has a spacious entrance area with oak floors that can serve as a cinema room and a space for parties and entertaining. The children's bedrooms and a study are also on the ground floor, as is a large kitchen at one end of the house, with bespoke banquettes in chestnut arranged around a dining table, which is Küchel's design.

The main living room is on the top floor of the house – a long, generous space that makes the most of the mesmerizing views of the lakes and the mountains through a long series of windows. A fireplace sits at one end, with a work and reading table at the other. The furniture includes contemporary pieces by Antonio Citterio and mid-century classics by Charles and Ray Eames, as well as more rustic items collected by Küchel over the years. The master bedroom and bathroom sit to one side of the living room, with a mezzanine library and television room above, overlooking the main living space.

Above all, this is a house that responds to the beauty of the location itself, making the most of the mountain scenery, while also seeking to respect the setting and context. 'In the winter you can just go out of the house with your skis and go cross-country or head up into the mountains,' Küchel says. 'And in the summer, you can go jogging or cycling, and the boys also love to go to the lake and fish. It is a very special location, between the mountains and the lake. It gives you energy, a sense of wellbeing.'

The front door was designed in sections and was partly inspired by the doorways found in the local barns, large enough to accommodate livestock or a hay cart. The main hallway is a generously scaled space that doubles as an additional reception room for entertaining.

The main sitting room is on the upper
level of the house, with a large fireplace
at one end and picture windows. The sofas
are by Antonio Citterio, as are the armchairs
covered in cowhide.

A mezzanine gallery, which serves as a
television room, den and library, looks
down onto the main sitting room.
The furniture is a mix of contemporary
pieces and mid-century design classics.

Above left and opposite The kitchen is a bespoke design by the owner, as is the chestnut dining table and banquette to one side.

Above, middle and right In the main living room, mountain photographs are hung alongside mid-century classics, such as this chair by Charles and Ray Eames.

Above The day bed in the mezzanine, high up in the eaves, is also a bespoke design; the table is from B&B Italia.

Opposite The master bedroom is on the upper storey, alongside the main sitting room, and leads out to a private balcony; the bed is a custom design.

LAUENEN RESIDENCE

Lauenen, Switzerland
Studio Seilern

The Swiss mountain hamlet of Lauenen has a calm, seductive character.
A few miles away from Gstaad, it sits at the end of a winding valley, where
the road ends and you can go no further in wintertime. The lack of any
through route, together with the natural beauty of the alpine setting, makes
this an idyllic spot to make a home. The village is populated by a sixteenth-
century church, a delight in itself, along with a modest collection of chalets
and farmhouses, which climb the lower slopes to either side of the valley.
In summer they sit alongside grazing pasture; in winter, the slopes are
deep in snow.

When architect Christina Seilern began thinking about designing
and building a home here for herself and her family, she started by looking
in detail at the history and architecture of chalets and farmhouses. She
undertook a careful study of the vernacular mountain architecture in the
region, trying to understand as much of the alpine heritage as she could.
Having grown up in the region herself – before studying and working in
the USA, and then settling in London – she was already at an advantage.

'We took photographs and studied the roofs, façades and windows, and
then organized the results by area,' says Seilern, who worked with Rafael
Viñoly for many years before founding her own architectural practice.
'Even though I grew up in Switzerland and could ski almost before I could
walk, I wanted to understand more about where the chalet as a typology
came from and what it really means as a building type, as well as why it is
so protected in this country by the planning regulations.'

This study influenced the design of her own chalet just outside Lauenen,
which is pushed gently into the hillside, with a picture-postcard panorama
of the mountains. Seilern created a masterplan for the site, which features
three separate chalets – including one for her mother – with a shared
underground car park and mechanical plant. But each building within
the triptych was designed individually, with Seilern's own house occupying
the central plot.

The timber-coated chalet has views across
the valley, the village of Lauenen and the mountains
opposite. The overhanging roofline shelters the
balconies and terraces around the house.

Collaborating with local architects Hauswirth Architektur, Seilern was obliged to work within the strict local building codes, yet sought to update the chalet concept and apply a more contemporary interpretation where she could. One key ambition was to maximize the number of windows, many of which lead onto adjoining terraces and balconies, to make the most of the light and to avoid the dark interiors found in many traditional alpine farmhouses.

The push for a more modern aesthetic finds far greater expression inside. Seilern opted to create a separate apartment at the top of the chalet, although this space can be easily integrated with the rest of the house at a later date. The lowest level, which is largely underground and tucked into the slope of the hill, was given over to a children's room, a guestroom and a family room. The spaces at the centre of the house, which have the best of the light and the views, are devoted to the main living spaces – the sitting room and dining area – which sit on one level within the fluid floor plan. The kitchen sits within a separate space to the rear, although a sense of connection to the dining area is maintained via an open serving hatch.

The use of materials establishes the contemporary approach, from textured timber to more 'artificial' materials, including the glass and exposed concrete, which reveal the heavy-duty shell of the building. Floors are in wide, whitened birch boards, while the ceilings and wall panelling are in a steamed pine that has been battered with mallets for greater texture. In the master bedroom, the ceilings and side wall are in exposed concrete, but the floors, panelling and bespoke bed are all in timber. A Hans Wegner 'Papa Bear' chair and bedside lights by Serge Mouille add another layer of interest, but the view itself is the main attraction. The bed faces out across the mountain panorama, and the balcony to one side looks towards the valley and the rising peaks.

This is a generously scaled, flexible home in a remarkable location, one that seeks to explore and update the long-established chalet tradition. 'We go to Lauenen as much as we can,' says Seilern. 'We love walking in the mountains, and the off-piste is great here – you can put skins on your skis and go off and walk for miles. Very soon you find that you are in the middle of nowhere.'

GROUND FLOOR

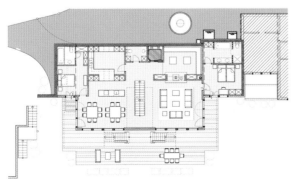

The master bedroom is bordered by a balcony, which frames a view of the mountains and snow-dusted pines.

The sitting room and dining room are
separated by the staircase, with its balustrades
of glass, which allows light to pass through
the main living spaces. The dining tables and
benches are bespoke designs by Seilern.

The sofa in the foreground is a Jasper
Morrison design for Vitra, while
the settee nearest the window is by
Rodolfo Dordoni for Cassina. The
armchairs are by Gerrit Rietveld.

The kitchen was designed as a separate
space to the dining room, although the
serving hatches offer a degree of connection.
The Boffi island in the dining room provides
a serving counter and bar; the lights above
the dining table are by Tom Dixon.

The custom-designed bed in the master suite is positioned for the mountain views. The bathroom alongside features a sculpted stone bath from Vaselli, while a bunk room provides space for the children and their guests.

CHALET LA TRANSHUMANCE

St-Martin-de-Belleville, France
Noé Duchaufour-Lawrance

The French word *transhumance* translates as 'pastures new'. It suggests – with a poetic touch – new beginnings and the embrace of fresh opportunities. Fittingly, this was the name of a restaurant in a small French alpine village, not far from St-Martin-de-Belleville, which Antoine Ernoult-Dairaine bought and reinvented as a new mountain home for himself and his family. He managed to persuade one of his favourite contemporary designers, Noé Duchaufour-Lawrance, to work on the conversion, bringing a dramatic modern aesthetic to the interiors of this traditionally built chalet of stone and timber.

Ernoult-Dairaine and his wife Isabelle have known the region for many years. They first began visiting Les Trois Vallées – which includes over 670km (416 miles) of ski runs and embraces the resorts of, among others, Courchevel, Méribel and Val Thorens – in the 1990s, when they discovered La Transhumance. They were instantly taken by the tranquil setting within a community that feels as though it is sitting on top of the world.

'We rented a chalet in Méribel for many years and used to ski here off-piste and then have lunch on the terrace under the sun,' says Ernoult-Dairaine, who lives and works in Paris for much of the year. 'The lunches were always joyful, and I fell in love with the place – quiet, sunny and with spectacular views. Each time I came, I would ask the owner to find me a house in the village.'

Eventually, a call came to say that a semi-derelict barn next to the restaurant was for sale, and Ernoult-Dairaine bought it straightaway. But the barn on its own proved to be too small for a family with four children. Some years later there was another call to say that La Transhumance itself was up for sale, and the family seized the chance at once.

Ernoult-Dairaine first became interested in Duchaufour-Lawrance's work when he bought a limited-edition 'Manta' desk, and took a keen interest in the designer's furniture from that point onwards. He managed to persuade Duchaufour-Lawrance to take on the reinvention of La Transhumance, beginning with the main living space at the top of the building and then, if all went well, the rest of the project.

The main body of the house is contained within a former restaurant; additional living space is provided in the former agricultural building next door, a little further down the slope.

This open-plan living space at the top of the house is the most striking and engaging floor of the building, enjoying the best of the light and the views. Here, Duchaufour-Lawrance created a sculpted interior, arranged around a fireplace that rises seamlessly from the concrete floor and continues upwards to the timber ceiling in the shape of an extraordinary ship-like funnel. The ceiling itself becomes a sinuous envelope that cascades down to the floor and transforms into fitted seating, while the custom kitchen units and dining table, made with milky Corian, stand out against the grey concrete and the organic tones of the larch and spruce, as well as the Vals stone used for the stairwell.

With the building pushed into the topography of the hillside and the adjoining barn even further down the slope, the rest of the house forms a procession of spaces leading down from the extraordinary family room that crowns La Transhumance. The designer was given carte blanche to create and curate rooms of particular originality and depth, each one of them an individual response to context and function; the barn now functions as a semi-autonomous space, well suited to guests.

The master suite has the feel of a fluid, ethereal cocoon, with a sinuous wall of grey timber forming a backdrop for the bed. This transforms into a sweeping screen that partially shelters the shower room alongside, morphing into a sink unit and storage cupboards. The rounded forms and rich variety of textures and finishes lend a fascinating sense of cohesion to the spaces, which are populated by many pieces of furniture designed by Duchaufour-Lawrance himself, along with lighting and art chosen through a process of creative collaboration between designer and client.

'We wanted him to produce something that would be immediately recognizable as Noé's work, so we did not provide a lot of requirements,' says Ernoult-Dairaine. 'But we also spent some time explaining our way of living, so that he could adapt the volumes and destinations of the rooms to suit us. The collaboration went into the smallest details, such as the photographs on the walls. It has been an exceptional project for us – a dialogue with a great artist.'

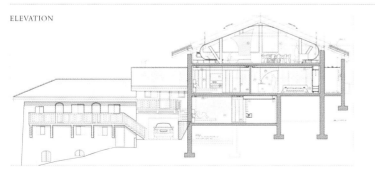

ELEVATION

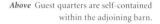
Above Guest quarters are self-contained within the adjoining barn.

Opposite A large picture window at the uppermost level of the house helps bring light down into the stairwell and onto the sculptural forms of the stairs themselves.

ELEVATION

The sculpted fireplace and chimney form
a dramatic centrepiece in the main living
space on the upper storey of the house.
The fitted sofas and the dining table are
also custom pieces by the architect.

While many of the fitted elements in the
open-plan living area are bespoke, pieces of
furniture designed by Duchaufour-Lawrance
include the benches and chair by the dining
table, produced by Ceccotti Collezioni, and
a 'Derby' armchair produced by Zanotta.

The use of timber and stone throughout the
house lends an organic character in keeping
with the rustic setting; sculpted Corian
and poured concrete floors reinforce the
contemporary aesthetic. The desk and chair
in the master bedroom are by Duchaufour-
Lawrance, produced by Ceccotti Collezioni.

PIOLET

Chamonix, France
Chevallier Architectes

The French mountain town of Chamonix sits within an extraordinary and often extreme landscape. The valley is bordered by the towering peaks of the Aiguilles Rouges and, in particular, the epic presence of Mont Blanc; at 4,810m (15,781 ft) high, it is the tallest peak in Europe. The first Winter Olympics were held here in 1924, and for many years the Aiguille du Midi cable car, rising to 3,842m (12,605 ft), was the highest of its kind in the world.

The town itself continues to attract a constant flow of climbers and extreme-sports enthusiasts, both in winter and summer. Many of the houses keep to a conventional chalet-style aesthetic, but there are signs of a fresher style evolving in residential design as contemporary architects such as Renaud Chevallier of Chevallier Architectes make their mark in the community.

As a third-generation architect based in Chamonix, Chevallier has a better understanding than most of the origins and character of mountain houses. When he acquired a small piece of land just outside the village, with the support of a friendly client for whom he had already built a neighbouring house, he was determined to try and update the idea of the traditional chalet. The new building that Chevallier built for himself pays its respects to the past, but is also decidedly modern, with a distinctive outline that combines horizontal slats of larch cladding with large windows, which frame the striking mountain views to either side.

The house sits upon the footprint of a dilapidated former farmhouse, and the architect had to work within both the outline of the original building and other restrictions imposed by the local building codes. 'I know the rules here so I was able to push the boundaries,' says Chevallier, who grew up in Chamonix, but studied in Paris and New York and has also worked in Italy and Mauritius. 'But at the same time I didn't want to create something that would disturb everything else around me. I haven't treated the larch, because I want it to turn grey over time and match the old farms and houses in the neighbourhood.'

The ground floor is an open-plan living space with picture windows and slate floors. A kitchen and dining area sit to one side, with seating arranged around a

The house has been sensitively designed, with careful thought given to its context and the ambition of establishing a constant sense of connection with the mountain landscape.

fireplace to the other. A timber trap door leads down to a cosy television room and evening lounge tucked away within a new basement level. Three bedrooms are on the floor above, with one of them doubling as a study. The master suite is a loft-like space right at the top of the house. Here, the 'bathroom' is contained within the bedroom itself, with a free-floating bath sitting by a window, looking out across the snow-dusted trees and to the rugged landscape beyond.

'I could have created two bedrooms on the top floor,' says Chevallier, 'but I wanted one large, luxurious space – like a loft apartment. Everything fitted is bespoke, but I also wanted to introduce colour and texture. The interiors are also designed to be flexible, so in a few years I might change some of the colours and bring in something else. So there is the capacity for the house to evolve and change.'

A contemporary aesthetic blends with traditional materials to create a home that is striking in its modernity, but also references the chalet tradition with elements such as the exposed beams and the wooden stairway, the one part of the house made with oak rather than larch. Above all, Chevallier's home is sensitively designed, with careful thought given to its context and the ambition of establishing a constant sense of connection with the mountain landscape.

'Building for yourself is a hard job,' Chevallier says. 'But I am a happy client, and if I had to do it all again then I would do exactly the same thing. We worked within all of the codes and restrictions of building in the mountains, but we were also able to turn the design in a fresh direction and shake things up. I wanted the house to point towards the future and explain that yes, we are in the mountains, but we are also in the twenty-first century.'

The building is situated within a quiet enclave on the edge of the town, where the snow-covered trees form a natural backdrop and the mountains are an epic presence to either side of the valley.

TOP FLOOR

GROUND FLOOR

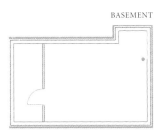

BASEMENT

The main living area on the ground floor is an open-plan space, combining the kitchen, dining area and sitting room. The seating area is arranged around a wood-burning stove and sliding doors that open onto a terrace.

A custom timber and steel staircase winds
its way up the house. The master bedroom
is contained on the uppermost floor of the
house and features an open-plan bathroom
with a sculptural, cocoon-shaped tub.

USINE GRUBEN

Gstaad, Switzerland
Antonie Bertherat-Kioes

Two vast generators sit alongside the kitchen in architect Antonie Bertherat-Kioes's mountain home. By the dining table, there is an electrical control panel that dates back to the early 1900s, now with an integrated fireplace. The house that Bertherat-Kioes shares with her husband Philippe and their four daughters was once a transformer station and station-master's house for the Montreux–Oberland Bernois railway, whose trains still stop at the platform outside. Now Bertherat-Kioes has transformed the building into a warm and characterful chalet home. But she could not bear the idea of parting with the generators, which sit at the heart of the house and remain a vital part of its identity.

Despite living and working in Geneva for the majority of the year, the architect and her family have a long-standing love of the mountains and are all skiers. They had a chalet at Valet Alpin, near Zermatt, but were drawn to Gstaad by the beauty of the landscape and the quiet charm of the surrounding valleys. They were looking for a small farm with buildings they could convert, but couldn't find anything suitable until they stumbled on the station house while trawling the Internet. Situated just outside Gstaad in a small hamlet, with farms and pasture all around, it was an unusual but tempting opportunity.

'It was just a small advert posted by an agent in Lausanne,' says Bertherat-Kioes, who worked with celebrated Austrian architect Günther Domenig before founding her own practice in 1998. 'But the agent didn't even come with me to look at the house. He said just go and ring the bell and the lady that used to live there would show me round. They didn't make a big fuss about it at all. Two developers were interested, but they wanted to turn the building into flats, so the train company sold it to us.'

Converting the station house presented quite a challenge. The section that housed the electrical equipment had been taken out of use in 1987, when a new transformer plant was built just across the railway tracks, but there was contamination from oil and pollution in the building and the garden, as well as a good deal of other mess and industrial detritus to be cleared away. Soil had

The house is a conversion of a former transformer station and the adjoining station-master's cottage; the railway line and the platform are still in daily use.

to be removed from the lower level of the structure, and in the generator hall the concrete floors were damaged and crumbling. This, however, created an opportunity to install underfloor heating, fed by a ground-source heat pump.

Bertherat-Kioes worked around the existing machinery to create a high-ceilinged entrance area, kitchen and dining space, bathed in natural light from tall, arched windows. She added a mezzanine at one end, accessed via the existing staircase, which now contains her study, looking out over the generator hall. Upstairs, another large industrial space was converted into a generously proportioned living room, with a new picture window at one end looking out across the valley towards Gstaad. Bertherat-Kioes wanted to ensure that the space felt warm and comfortable, so created a seating area and a fireplace at one end, and a separate seating zone planned around a library at the opposite end of the room. She designed a bespoke fabric for the walls, and blended contemporary furniture with mid-century pieces and striking artworks.

Underneath the living room, the architect designed a generous master suite. Here, the greatest challenge was how to design a private bathroom that felt connected to the bedroom, but without swallowing up the few valuable windows looking out across the mountain vista. The solution was a crafted timber box that sits at the centre of the room, with the sleeping and dressing areas to either side. A sculpted Boffi bath sits to one side of the bathroom, while an internal window borrows natural light from the bedroom beyond. The adjoining station-master's house has been converted into contemporary chalet-style quarters with bedrooms for the children, their friends and guests.

The result is a highly individual home, where the industrial character of the generator hall has been balanced by rooms that are defined by an organic sense of warmth and material texture, with an eclectic but sophisticated mix of furnishings and art. It is also beautifully situated for appreciating the landscape and making the most of the winter sports, with the train to the slopes stopping right on the family's doorstep.

The dining area and kitchen are located in the old generator hall, alongside the remaining machinery and the control unit. The dining table and chairs are by George Nakashima; the 'Help' artwork is by Christian Robert-Tissot.

FLOOR PLAN

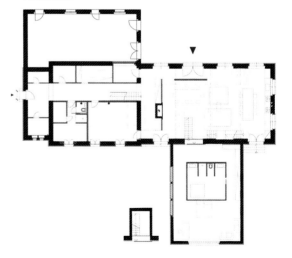

A new window was added in the sitting room, looking down into the valley and across to the mountains opposite. The sofa is by India Mahdavi, while the bowl armchair is a Jean Royère design; the two armchairs by the smaller window are also by Royère.

The large artwork in the sitting room is
by Ugo Rondinone, while the fabric on the
walls is a custom design by Arpin. The stools
are Finnish, and the coffee table is another
design produced by India Mahdavi.

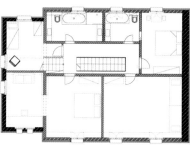

SECOND FLOOR

The master bathroom is contained within
a crafted timber box that floats within the
master suite; the bath is by Boffi and the
vintage chair alongside is by Hans Wegner.

BASEMENT

ATTIC

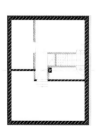
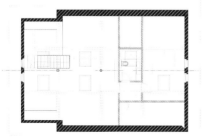

The children's bunk room, bedrooms and guest suites are located in the old station-master's house, next to the generator building. The bunk beds are a custom design by the architect; the elephant photograph is by Balthasar Burkhard.

SUGAR BOWL HOUSE

Norden, California, USA
John Maniscalco Architecture

The mountains have always played a large part in the lives of interior designer Maca Huneeus and her husband, vintner Agustin Francisco Huneeus, who first met at the Chilean ski resort of La Parva. The couple and their five daughters are all strong skiers, and the family have made regular trips to the California ski resort of Sugar Bowl, not far from Lake Tahoe, for many years. Founded in the late 1930s on the slopes of Mt Lincoln and Mt Judah, Sugar Bowl is blessed with some of the best skiing in the state, and is one of the closest resorts to San Francisco, where the family live for much of the year.

'Sugar Bowl is very much a word-of-mouth kind of place,' says Huneeus, who largely grew up in Chile, then came to California to finish her studies and later founded her own design studio. 'Some family friends first invited us, and we immediately fell in love with it. We rented different houses at Sugar Bowl for years and tried to buy something, but it didn't work out. Eventually we were very lucky to end up with a lot in the old village, where we could build a new house – it was the best of both worlds.'

In the resort's historic village, access is by gondola and there are no cars. Residents can ski from their front doors to the ski lifts, and the setting is secluded, tranquil and rich in natural beauty, with pine trees creating a verdant backdrop. Huneeus turned to architect John Maniscalco, who she had already worked with on the family home in San Francisco, to design the building.

'When I first saw the site, it was still covered in six feet of snow,' Maniscalco says. 'Several hours of traipsing through drifts up to my waist gave me an appreciation of the severity of the conditions, while the combination of filtered light through the trees and views of the mountain was particularly striking. The massive snow pack around the houses at Sugar Bowl creates dark, buried floors at the base, and treacherous entrances that require constant clearing. So we knew that these kind of practicalities would be primary drivers for the design.'

Architect and client decided very early on that the house – which sits in a clearing among the pines – should be elevated on a 2.4m (8 ft) concrete plinth to raise the main body of the building up above the winter snow. The lower

This house among the woods is raised off the ground on a robust plinth, so that the building can still be accessed with ease in the winter months when the snow level is high.

level of the house holds the entrance, via a series of timber steps, as well as a large bunk room for the children, plus guest accommodation, a boot room and utility spaces. The living spaces all sit on the upper level, with the best of the views. An open-plan living and dining area sits at the heart of the house, feeding out onto a sheltered deck. The kitchen sits to one side of the building, with the master suite situated at the other.

'More than anything, we wanted the house to be simple, functional and quiet, but also warm and refined,' says Huneeus. 'I also wanted to "feel" the mountain at all times through the big windows, and see the trees and the landscape. But we didn't want a huge house that would accumulate dust and spider webs. If Agustin and I ever go up on our own, the house doesn't feel too big. We can just heat the upstairs, and you almost feel as though you are in a separate house, without dealing with the downstairs area at all.'

Cedar siding and ceilings help soften the building, along with timber floors upstairs and wooden panelling for the stairway, which features a dramatic picture window looking out across the tree canopy. Many fitted elements, including the kitchen and bunk beds, are custom designs by the architect and client, who collaborated closely on the interiors. A mix of contemporary pieces, vintage finds and textiles sourced by Huneeus brings character and personality into the home. The house sees use over the summer, when the children participate in the Sugar Bowl summer camp, but it really comes into its own during the winter months for ski weekends and holidays, including Christmas and New Year.

'It is a very special place, and we love it in summer when it's so quiet and beautiful,' Huneeus says. 'We come a lot in the winter, and because there are no cars the kids can wander from house to house and we ski everywhere – even to a friend's place for lunch or coffee. You park your car in the garage on a Friday night, go up in the gondola and don't see the car again until Sunday evening. It's very free, and you are right in the middle of nature. It is a real pleasure.'

REAR ELEVATION

FRONT ELEVATION

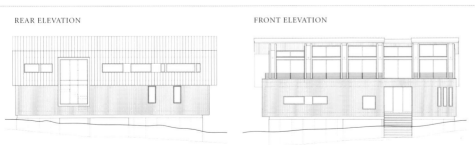

The staircase features a vast window looking out onto the forest, as well as a custom-designed window seat. The chandelier overhead is by Bocci.

The main living spaces are positioned on the upper storey of the house, creating a wonderful vantage point for looking out into the trees. The sofas are by Molteni, while the coffee tables are from BoConcept.

The dining area sits to one side of the
open-plan living space; the dining table
and mirror are custom-designed pieces
by Huneeus's own design company. The
kitchen is also a bespoke design by Huneeus,
with ceiling lights by Jonathan Adler.

Above The master suite and bathroom are on the upper storey, next to the main living spaces.

Right The children's room and guest accommodation are on the lower floor; the bunk beds are another custom design by Huneeus and the bedside lamps are by Jonathan Adler.

VILLA

VILLA

Introduction

One of the most influential houses of the twentieth century is set within a rugged hillside landscape of particular beauty. Frank Lloyd Wright's Fallingwater, in the Appalachian mountains of Pennsylvania, sits alongside Bear Run, a tributary of the Youghiogheny River, with the building cantilevered out over the cascading water. The house was commissioned by Pittsburgh department store owner Edgar J. Kaufmann, for a rural property where his family had owned a holiday cabin for many years.

'He loved the site where the house was built and liked to listen to the waterfall,' Wright said of the project, 'so that was the prime motive in the design. I think you can hear the waterfall when you look at the design.'

The house was, above all, a response to the site itself and the surrounding landscape. The architecture seeks to work with the topography and the slope of the rocky site, rather than attempting to shape or force the land into an accommodation. It is a prime example of what Wright described as an 'organic' approach to architecture, with the word referring not so much to the materials – although the building did include locally quarried stone, as well as a good deal of concrete – but the way in which a building should be integrated into a site with sensitivity and subtlety.

'When organic architecture is properly carried out,' Wright observed, 'no landscape is ever outraged by it, but is always developed by it. The good building makes the landscape more beautiful than it was before the building was built.'

As a philosophy of architectural design, this 'organic' approach has been profoundly influential. This has certainly been the case in recent decades, when much greater thought has been given to environmental concerns, questions of sustainability and protecting the landscape. Within a rural mountain context, where a house may assume particular prominence by virtue of its isolation and hillside position, the need for a sensitive, considered approach becomes of special importance. Building within settings of great natural beauty clearly carries with it a special responsibility.

Contemporary architects and designers have responded to the challenge of building modern homes in the mountains and hills in very different and varied ways. Some have sought to reinterpret vernacular ideas and local traditions with fresh thinking, as seen in the design of many modern cabins and chalets. Others have developed more radical and innovative strategies, as seen in Villa Vals (pp.

> '[Kaufmann] loved the site where the house was built and liked to listen to the waterfall ... I think you can hear the waterfall when you look at the design.'
>
> FRANK LLOYD WRIGHT

182–91), in Switzerland, designed by Bjarne Mastenbroek of SeARCH. Here, wishing to respect and preserve the mountain landscape as much as possible, Mastenbroek pushed his house into the hillside itself, so that much of the building is essentially contained within the slope and the impact of the villa much reduced. Yet at the same time the house frames the landscape with great care and attention, forming a strong relationship between inside and outside space.

It is this dual task of working with the landscape while establishing clear and constant connections between interior and exterior that lies at the heart of the design of the modern mountain villa. In the Californian resort of Northstar, near Lake Tahoe, architects Marmol Radziner created a home that adapts itself to the sloping site (pp. 218–27), while also offering a series of terraces and outdoor living spaces within a response to the mountain panorama. The vineyards that hug the hills above Stuttgart directly inspired the design of UNStudio's Haus am Weinberg (pp. 244–51), which seeks to mirror the experience of being within this sloping landscape, while also providing a direct link between the house and the surrounding countryside.

Clearly, a mountain site does offer a particular perspective upon the landscape, and one that should be accentuated within the design of the house. Toshiko Mori's Cloudline (pp. 200–7) and Alberto Campo Baeza's Olnick Spanu House (pp. 208–17) both in New York's Hudson Valley, make the most of prominent vantage points on the prow of a hill to create powerful belvederes that invite the landscape right into the house. The panorama is the great reason for building the house in the first place, and this is never forgotten.

But this is not to deny the artistry and originality to be found within the architecture of the mountain home. While context and setting are respected and an intrinsic part of the design process, a hillside home will – inevitably – have a degree of prominence and drama by virtue of its isolated position within the landscape. For architects and artists this creates a unique invitation, as seen in the collaboration between architects HHF and Chinese artist Ai Weiwei to the design the Tsai Residence (pp. 172–81) upon a hilltop in Upstate New York – a building of sculptural beauty and intensity. The mountain villa, then, is both an extraordinary opportunity and a particular responsibility.

TSAI RESIDENCE

Ancram, New York, USA
HHF Architects with Ai Weiwei

Sitting atop a picture-perfect hill in New York's Hudson Valley, the Tsai
Residence has the look of an abstract sculpture placed within the landscape.
Formed from four interconnected cubes, coated in corrugated aluminium,
the house seems enigmatic and curious, like a piece of land art. From certain
angles the building seems largely closed, rather like the agricultural silos that
pepper the region. If the sculpted form suggests an artist's hand, then it's a fair
assumption, as this is the first and only house in America by Chinese artist,
sculptor and architectural designer Ai Weiwei, designed with HHF Architects.
This combination of art-world figurehead, a Swiss architectural practice and
clients who mix Asian–American and European heritage has given rise to a
unique home full of surprises.

   Although the exterior appears solid, enclosed and semi-industrial, stepping
into the house reveals a warm and generous interior with open-plan and
double-height spaces contrasting with more intimate retreats. Discreetly
placed openings connect with the landscape, while a series of clerestory
windows and skylights introduce a rich quality of natural light. Natural
materials such as timber floors and brick fireplaces help warm this house of
art, dominated by pieces by Weiwei himself and other Chinese artists, such
as Cai Guo-Qiang, whose vast gunpowder painting dominates the living area.

   It was the need for space to accommodate these large-scale artworks that
gave the clients – an investment manager and a fashion designer – the impetus
to build their own country home. With 16 hectares (40 acres) of land and few
planning restrictions (apart from a height limitation based upon the ladder of
the local fire truck), the site was a great temptation. The couple knew Weiwei's
work well, and were introduced by their New York art dealer. The artist is
known for an intuitive approach to architecture, which he sees as closely
bound up with art itself. His buildings include the Three Shadows Photography
Art Centre, a composition of carefully crafted grey-brick structures, and the
'Bird's Nest' Olympic Stadium, both in Beijing, the latter a collaboration with
architects Herzog & de Meuron.

The house sits upon a prominent hillside site
with far-reaching views and woodland to the
rear. At one end of the house, a large veranda
serves as an outdoor sitting and dining space.

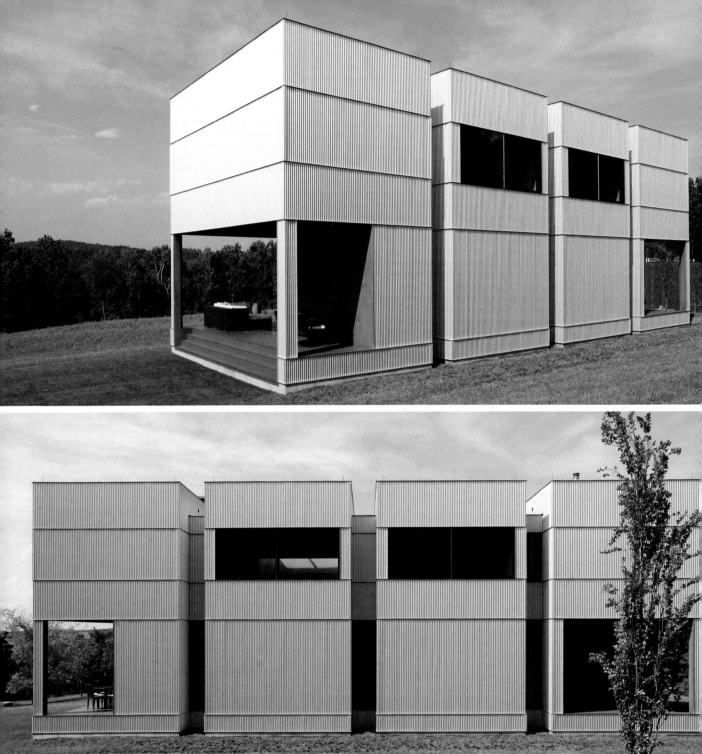

'We started collecting Chinese art in 2002 and became more and more enthralled by it, so that it became a passion of ours,' say the clients. 'Weiwei is mostly known as an artist, but he is also a name in architecture, so he became the conceptual designer and the inspiration behind the house. We just wanted enough wall space for art and three bedrooms and fireplaces, but we didn't set out many requests. We both believe that if you hire someone like Ai Weiwei, then you should respect their vision.'

Weiwei had already worked with the Basel-based practice HHF Architects on a number of projects, so the relationship was already well established. Initial conversations began without either artist or architects having visited the site. 'We knew that this was a large piece of land with a hilly situation,' says architect Simon Frommenwiler. 'The house began as an abstract piece sitting on top of the hill, a sculptural object that might be a little bit out of scale. Weiwei is interested in the power of space, and how people live in the building and walk through it. It's about the basic idea of the home, but he's not trained as an architect, so he does need someone to work with on his ideas.'

While the clients were initially interested in the idea of maximizing the links between the interiors and the surrounding landscape, Weiwei looked for a more insular approach with echoes of traditional Chinese architecture. The windows are subtly placed, allowing edited glimpses of the countryside, and the use of skylights and high windows in the double-height living spaces allows for an indirect light that helps protect the artworks on the walls. Along with the minimalist approach to the interiors, this lends the house a gallery-like flavour.

Oak floors, fireplaces and walls of soft, grey brick all help to add warmth and texture; the Boffi kitchen, another key consideration, is treated as the heart of the home. Guests are granted privacy with a bedroom on the ground floor, set apart from the main, semi-open-plan living spaces, while a master bedroom and nursery are on the floor above. There's also a library – with bespoke shelving and a fireplace making it a seductive space to work from home – as well as a salt-water swimming pool nearby and a new studio, which formed a later addition to the site.

From the outside, the house is divided into four neat bays, with the veranda tucked into the outline of the building at one end and the entrance porch at the other.

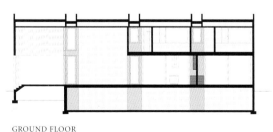

GROUND FLOOR

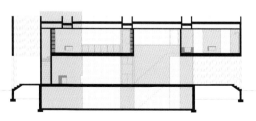

FIRST FLOOR

The main living spaces on the ground floor are interconnected, with a free-flowing relationship between the kitchen and zones for sitting and dining. Skylights and clerestory windows, as well as a number of smaller window openings, offer a rich quality of light and create a gallery-like atmosphere.

Above Artworks by Ai Weiwei include the twin table sculpture and a series of vases in the library; the portrait of Lenin in the guest bedroom is by Li Dafang.

Opposite The painting above the B&B Italia sofa is by Cai Guo-Qiang, one of the artist's gunpowder works.

Above The pool terrace and the veranda, with an outdoor fireplace, offer views out across the rolling hills.

Opposite The swimming pool is a crisp line upon the hillside.

VILLA VALS

Vals, Switzerland
SeARCH

Building a new home within a landscape as precious and dramatic as
the mountain valleys of Graubünden brings with it a particular sense of
responsibility. Here, the beauty of the mountains and nature itself is everything,
and especially so within the alpine village of Vals, around 1,250m (4,100 ft) up
at the end of a valley, where the slopes form picturesque panoramas dotted with
farmers' barns for wintering livestock. This is the setting for Peter Zumthor's
thermal baths and hotel, as well as the famous source for bottled mineral water,
yet it is the natural beauty of the Alps that remains the prime draw.

Dutch architect Bjarne Mastenbroek, having fallen in love with the area over
a number of years, decided to build a new house for himself and his family
here, while seeking to protect and preserve the surrounding landscape as much
as possible. The solution was to push the building into a sloping hillside, so that
the structure seeks to become a part of the topography, rather than struggling
against it. 'We design buildings that respond to the existing situation, to the
context and the landscape,' says Mastenbroek, founder of SeARCH, a practice
based in Amsterdam. 'At Vals, we wanted to preserve the purity of the land
between the existing houses, while designing a house that was environmentally
efficient and sustainable.'

A period stone-and-timber barn to one side of the site was restored
and preserved as a gatehouse to the villa, with a new tunnel leading from
its basement level into the main building. The house itself was created by
excavating 11m (36 ft) deep into the slope and building a retaining wall made
of concrete to the rear. The living spaces, arranged over two-and-a-half floors,
were then slotted into this void, which was enclosed within a concave stone
façade leading out to a recessed terrace. The entire building sits neatly within
the hillside, with avalanche nets around the rim of the circular opening to
protect it from heavy snowfall. A series of windows puncture the façade and
introduce a surprisingly rich quality of natural light throughout.

'The villagers assumed that the house would be small and dark, but that's
not the way it works,' says Mastenbroek, who collaborated on the design with

The villa is accessed via a secret underground
tunnel that runs from a neighbouring barn.
From the villa itself and its terrace, the view
is of the mountain slopes, dotted with farmers'
huts and livestock sheds.

architect Christian Müller. 'Many traditional farmhouses here are much darker because they have smaller windows. This house faces southeast with 50m² (538 sq ft) of triple-glazing on the façade, while the house itself is not deep. So it's a lot lighter than traditional chalets, and each room has a spectacular view. The edge of the hole in the hillside actually frames the view as if it were a painting.'

The lower level of the house holds the main sitting room to one side and a guest suite at the other, while at the centre of the building the kitchen and dining area, a few steps further down, sit on the same level as the semicircular terrace outside. The stairs are to the rear, leading up to another three bedrooms. As well as many integrated pieces of furniture, the furnishings include some mid-century classics and more contemporary work by a number of Dutch designers, including Hella Jongerius and Marcel Wanders. There is a curated sophistication to the mix, but the atmosphere is warm, welcoming and calm.

Anxious to make the house as sustainable as possible, Mastenbroek embraced a series of environmentally friendly solutions for preserving heat and energy. By embedding the house in the slope, the surrounding soil adds to the super-insulated specification of the building, as well as doing away with the need for the standard pitched roof, which graces most houses in the region. The architects also opted for a ground-source heat pump, which feeds radiant underfloor heating, and takes its electricity from the hydroelectric station at the Zervreila reservoir. The decision to rent the house to paying guests for part of the year, along with using the villa as a family retreat, was also grounded in the desire to have a sustainable home that would see constant, year-round use.

'The house really does appeal to people,' says Mastenbroek. 'It gives you that feeling of being comforted – it's something that runs quite deep within us. The house is much more relaxing than we ever hoped for, and because the house is focused on one view of a hilltop across the valley, you do feel as though you are in the middle of nowhere, even though the house is part of the village. It's a great combination, and it's wonderful to feel as though you are alone with this incredible view.'

FLOOR PLAN

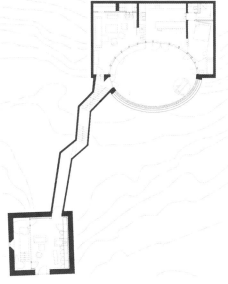

Above right Shifts in floor level mark the boundary between the sitting room and the kitchen/dining room adjoining the terrace.

Opposite The bespoke dining table in zebrano wood was designed by the architects and the chairs are vintage designs by Cor Alons.

The main sitting room features a blend of mid-century classics, such as the Hans Wegner 'Papa Bear' chair, and contemporary designs, including armchairs by Hella Jongerius and lighting from Moooi.

Above Other bedrooms, including a bunk room, are located on the upper level of the house, with views out from a series of irregular windows piercing the stone façade (see overleaf).

Opposite The bedroom on the ground floor includes vaulted cardboard shelving by Studio JVM and a wood-burning stove; the chair is a Marcel Wanders design.

HAUS AM BERG ISEL

Bregenz, Austria
Elmar Ludescher Architect

The city of Bregenz, where the mountains meet the waters of Lake Constance, has many charms. This is the capital of Vorarlberg, a part of Austria famed for a progressive and sustainable approach to contemporary architecture, and home to Peter Zumthor's acclaimed art gallery, the Kunsthaus Bregenz. It also sits on one of the pivotal axis points of Europe, close to the borders of both Germany and Switzerland, giving the community an outward-looking, international context. But it is the natural beauty of Bregenz and its hinterland that impresses most. Here, in the Pfänder foothills at the edge of the city, architect Elmar Ludescher designed and built a home for himself, partner Angelika Stefan and their young daughter. Arranged over three levels, the house makes the most of the views across the slopes and the city itself.

'We wanted the kitchen and dining area to be right at the top, so that we get the best of the views,' says Ludescher, who grew up in and around Bregenz and studied at the Academy of Fine Arts in Vienna. 'The lower ground floor is very introverted, the ground floor is quite open, but the top floor is like a bird's nest – a space up in the canopy of the trees. On a clear day you can see all the way to the city of Konstanz, right on the other side of the lake.'

The house sits upon a sloping site, with a steep drop to one side, falling away to an alpine stream that winds its way downwards to the lake. The steel and concrete framework was pushed into the hillside and coated in a layer of glass and larch. Sliding timber shutters coat the upper storey of the side of the house closest to the street, providing privacy and a brise soleil. On the other side, the main staircase is cradled within a timber outrigger that projects outwards from the main body of the building.

The lowermost, basement level is a largely self-contained space, suitable for guests, holding its own kitchen, bedroom and living room. The ground floor features the main entrance and a large, open-plan sitting room and studio, with a generously scaled custom desk and floor-to-ceiling glass, looking out across the city. By the entrance area there is a substantial veranda that also serves as a car port, sheltered by the cantilevered form of the storey above. The master

The cantilevered terrace on the upper level hovers above the hillside and a stream that runs alongside the house; the staircase is contained within a timber flank that projects outwards from the main body of the building.

suite, a bedroom for the couple's daughter Paulina and the open-plan kitchen and dining area all sit on the upper level. This fluid family space leads out to a roof terrace, which is sheltered by a canopy formed by the projecting roofline but pierced with a circular, open skylight.

'We have a curtain on a track around the roof terrace that we can use in the summertime for shade,' Ludescher explains. 'So you can close the space to create an outdoor room, and then the only full sunlight that you have comes from the circle in the roof. I love the way that the atmosphere of the house changes from winter to summer, when you have the sound of the curtains moving in the breeze and the sunlight filtering into the house through the wooden slats.'

The main family room has an organic sense of warmth lent by the use of silver fir, with a custom kitchen and a self-designed dining table in oak, surrounded by chairs designed by Max Bill. To one side of the space Ludescher added a built-in den for his daughter, with a day bed and a sliding door that can be used for greater privacy and to close off the nearby stairwell. 'This is the best space in the house,' says Angelika. 'Whenever children come and visit they always go to the den; they can put up a curtain and make it into a theatre and dance and perform.'

For Ludescher, who has his own practice in Bregenz, but also often collaborates on larger projects with his friend and colleague Philip Lutz (see Ferienhaus Girardi; pp. 22–31), the house represents a key element in his evolution as an architect and designer. It is a tailored home, with a design that perfectly corresponds to the rituals of daily living, as well as offering a good deal of flexibility.

'The house is very different from summer to winter,' Angelika explains. 'We even change the furniture according to the seasons. From July onwards we are in the garden, but from September we use the roof terrace and it feels like we are living in a boat moored on the hill. So it was very important to us to have both the terrace and the garden and have these choices.'

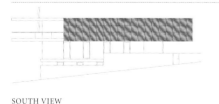

SOUTH VIEW

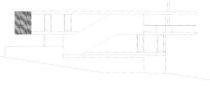

NORTH VIEW

Above A circular skylight above the terrace provides a glimpse of the sky, while a curtain on tracks can be pulled across to shade this outdoor dining room in the summer months.

Opposite A sliding wall of lattice timber creates a flexible brise soleil, which shelters the living spaces on the upper level and protects a small ship-style deck at the side of the house.

Above The latticed timber brise soleil on
the outside of the building also protects
the bedrooms on the upper storey.

Left The main living space on the upper
level consists of an open-plan kitchen and
dining room, with a bespoke table by the
architect and dining chairs by Max Bill.

The sitting room and a studio are positioned within a large and open space at mid-level, with floor-to-ceiling windows and views out across the woodland, which populates the hillside across the nearby ravine.

CLOUDLINE

Hudson Valley, New York, USA
Toshiko Mori

Cloudline is a house that seems to float above the landscape. Perched upon a small plateau, the building sits high up on a hillside, with a steep bluff falling away below and woodland to the rear. The countryside spreads out below the house, within an epic panorama that stretches all the way to Albany and the Catskills. The forest here is green and verdant, and the only traces of town and city lie in the far distance. This is an escapist location, where the only sounds are birdsong and the rustle of the breeze in the nearby trees.

This notion of a floating home is enhanced by the way that the upper level of the building, holding four bedrooms, projects over the lower storey, forming a dramatic cantilever that pushes out into the void, creating an elevated viewing deck from which to savour the rural vista. Yet the upper floor of the house, clad in textured aluminium panels, offers a greater sense of mass and solidity than the relative transparency of the ground floor, adding to the idea of a building that seems to somehow defy gravity.

'As architects, gravity is our fate, and we work with and against it,' says architect Toshiko Mori. 'So of course the house is about the defiance of gravity and our wish to be free of our earthbound destiny. The cantilever element is fundamental to the success and design of the building. The intent was to provoke a sensation of a mass being lifted by an unlikely and ethereal material.'

The house was commissioned by a Manhattan-based art dealer who had known the area for some years, and already owned a studio space in a nearby town. The new house, as well as responding to an extraordinary site, needed to accommodate an art collection that included pieces by Antony Gormley, Richard Long, Peter Liversidge and Rebecca Horn. The processional nature of the entrance area heightens a sense of anticipation as one approaches the main body of the house. The entry hallway has a tunnel-like character, with walls of bare concrete to one side and aluminium panels to the other, illuminated from above by a modest rectangular skylight. Emerging from this tunnel one arrives in a brighter, secondary entrance, dominated by a large painting by Birgir Andrésson, which reads 'all this and heaven as well'.

The house is positioned on a promontory looking out across the valley below; a sculpture by British artist Antony Gormley shares the view.

The plan of the ground floor is fluid, with an easy-flowing circulation and very few solid doorways. Yet at the same time each space in the house is clearly defined, with its own specific function. The main living room sits at the front of the building, with a dining room to one side and a more intimately scaled lounge to the other. These three principal spaces enjoy the best of the views. The kitchen, with space enough for a breakfast table, is positioned to the back of the house with windows looking out into the woods. The choice of furniture includes Scandinavian classics by Poul Kjærholm and Arne Jacobsen, as well as bespoke pieces, such as the dining table designed by Peter Superti and the architect herself.

The upper storey contains the four bedrooms, including the master suite at the front of the building, with a private balcony to one side. A generously scaled, custom-designed library sits at the centre of this floor of the house, with carefully controlled light levels to protect the book collection. The overhang helps lend a degree of shade to the outdoor terrace in the summer, while the grounds around the house also play host to a number of sculptures and other artworks. A life-size figure by Antony Gormley looks out over the edge of the bluff and a playful piece of signage by Peter Liversidge reading 'the thrill of it all' (see p. 6) sits among the woodland trees to the rear.

Yet clearly it is the site itself, and its genius loci, which has the greatest sense of presence here. 'The site does have a very special aura,' says Mori. 'We felt that this must be a native sanctuary site, which celebrates the idea of "lift" and the transcendental sensation you get through the observation of the landscape. What pleases me most is that the family love the house, and that they are still finding joy and an infinite variety of surprises with the building and its setting.'

MAIN LEVEL

UPPER LEVEL

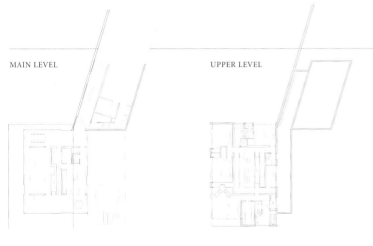

The main living spaces are positioned at the front of the house, making the most of the views down into the valley; the two chairs in the morning room are by Marc Newson and the sofa is by Poul Kjærholm.

In the main sitting room, the sofas are from
Minotti and the coffee tables are by Poul
Kjærholm. Artworks include pieces by Callum
Innes, Marina Abramovic and Los Carpinteros.

The master bedroom upstairs features floor-to-ceiling windows and a balcony for appreciating the extraordinary open vista; the chaise longue is a Poul Kjærholm design and the round table and twin armchairs by the fireplace are vintage Brazilian pieces.

OLNICK SPANU HOUSE

Garrison, New York, USA
Alberto Campo Baeza

The Hudson River and its hinterland have a powerful natural beauty and have long attracted artists, painters and photographers. Thomas Cole, Frederic Edwin Church and other painters of the romantic Hudson Valley School were fascinated by the dramatic resonance of the landscape here. This is particularly true of regions such as Dutchess, Putnam and Columbia Counties, where the water course carves its way through the rugged hills that rise up to either side and form a striking vantage point over the river.

The Hudson is also, of course, one of the great nineteenth-century trading routes. The Erie Canal opened up the port of New York to the Great Lakes via the Hudson Valley and the big cities of Albany and Buffalo. Ships still navigate the river and train routes make their way along both banks of the Hudson. Watching this constant passing traffic can be almost as engaging as the landscape itself.

Perched on a hillside near Garrison, in Putnam County, Spanish architect Alberto Campo Baeza has created a home that forms a perfect platform for appreciating this vista. It is a building that embodies a striking contrast between a largely enclosed podium at its lower level, with carefully edited views of the landscape from its lens-like windows, topped by a light and almost ethereal glass pavilion. This transparent pavilion, floating upon the heavy mass of the concrete plinth, is a belvedere that gazes out over the river valley below.

'I fell in love with the site straight away,' says Campo Baeza, who was commissioned by a family of art collectors. 'I knew immediately what kind of house I should make here. The house tries to understand the site, and to underline and frame the views. At the top of it, you feel as if you are on a magic carpet and entering the landscape itself – or as if the landscape is coming to meet you.'

The clients had owned the hillside property for many years and wanted a new home that would accentuate the relationship between the property and the Hudson Valley. The building sits within a clearing in the woodlands, surrounded by trees, and rests on a modest plateau, perched upon the high

The upper storey of the building is a glass pavilion, with a generously scaled terrace alongside, with views down to the Hudson River; the pool is positioned within a plateau of grassland nearby.

slope of the hill. A long driveway winds its way through the woods to this clearing, where visitors step downwards to a processional entrance in the lower part of the house. A large entry hall has the feel of a gallery, playing host to part of the owners' art collection, with Italian artists of the Arte Povera movement particularly well represented in a curated collection that also includes glassware and ceramics. Bedrooms, a library and utility spaces are all positioned on the lower storey of the building.

The upstairs is devoted to the principal living spaces of the house, set within a transparent pavilion paved with travertine that carries through to the long terrace alongside, where the cantilevered roof provides a degree of shade and helps shelter the interiors from the high summer sun. The central section of the pavilion is open plan, with a dining area to one side and a seating area to the other. A more intimate lounge sits at one end of the structure, partially divided from the central living space by a single, monolithic bespoke unit that holds a secondary spiral staircase, a bar, a fireplace and shelving. A similar monolith at the opposite end of the pavilion shelters the main staircase and forms part of a semi-separate kitchen.

The furniture is a mix of contemporary pieces and mid-century designs by the likes of Alvar Aalto, Poul Kjærholm and Mies van der Rohe. There is a soothing purity to the belvedere, with the green canopy of the trees to one side and the open view of the river valley to the other. 'The house is very calm and serene,' says Campo Baeza. 'It transmits a sense of serenity.'

A swimming pool sits at one remove to the main house, placed upon a green lawn at the same level as the upper storey of the building. The verdant greenery of the woodland and lawn stand in contrast to the crisp outline of the house itself and its geometric precision. Seen from down in the valley below, the villa appears as a considered composition of rectangular forms, softened and sheltered by the surrounding trees.

SECTION

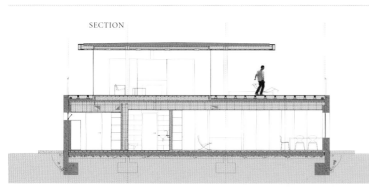

The lower level of the house, containing the bedrooms, a library and a central gallery, forms a more enclosed and insular storey with edited openings to the exterior; the fountain is by Massimo Bartolini.

Olnick Spanu House   211

Above A separate lounge is at the far end
of the pavilion, with chairs by Mies van der
Rohe and Poul Kjærholm; the globe artwork
is by Michelangelo Pistoletto.

Opposite The central portion of the pavilion
contains an open-plan seating area and a
dining zone; the dining table is by Pierluigi
Cerri, the chairs are by Mies van der Rohe
and the white armchairs are by Alvar Aalto.

Above Two partitions with twin staircases partially divide the upper pavilion into three distinct segments, with the lounge at one end and the kitchen at the other.

Opposite In the library on the lower floor the table and chairs are Alvar Aalto designs; the artwork is by Alighiero Boetti.

Among the many mid-century items of furniture in the house are chair designs by Eero Aarnio and Poul Kjærholm.

In the master bedroom, the reclining chair
and ottoman are by Charles and Ray Eames,
while artworks include pieces by Alighiero
Boetti, above the bed, and Domenico Bianchi.

SCHROEDER COURT

Lake Tahoe, California, USA
Marmol Radziner

The mountain resort of Northstar has its attractions all year round. In the summer there's hiking, mountain biking and golf, while in the winter this is prime ski and snowboard territory, with over ninety runs and nineteen lifts. But perhaps the greatest draw is the beauty of the landscape itself, with the wooded hillsides and mountain peaks of Placer County, as well as the alpine waters of Lake Tahoe, sitting on the border between California and Nevada.

Architects Marmol Radziner were commissioned to build not one but two houses within a mountain community not far from Northstar. They were designed for two families – friends of one another – who live in Los Angeles and wanted a countryside escape in the Sierra Nevada mountains for weekends and holidays throughout the year. Schroeder Court was built upon a rugged, sloping parcel of land that drops off to a creek in the valley below. The hillside site looks out to views southwards, taking in the ski runs of Lookout Mountain, and also benefits from the southern light. It is a perfect position for appreciating the landscape as it shifts and changes through the seasons.

With street access to the north, the house was oriented upon the hill to take best advantage of the views and the sunlight, with the main living spaces and adjoining terraces looking out over the panorama. The architects worked with the natural topography, slotting the building into the hillside in two sections connected by a slim, glass-encased bridge. The main body of the house is two storeys, with living space below and guest bedrooms and children's bunk rooms on the upper floor, while a satellite building sits a little further down the slope and contains the master bedroom, with a study tucked underneath.

'The clients wanted that sense of separation,' says architect Ron Radziner. 'Putting the smaller building on part of the site that steps down the hill was a way to create some privacy. Because it's south-facing, the window openings are set back pretty far, so that they can be protected from the sun. When you are in that bedroom space, you really feel like you are floating in the trees, with the way the space hovers above the ground. The roof tilts upwards both here and in the main house, so you get the entire mountain view.'

The wooded hillsides provide a seductive backdrop; the master bedroom and a study are contained within a smaller satellite building positioned alongside the main body of the house.

Both buildings employ a natural and organic palette of materials. Clark Fork Ledge, a type of fieldstone, was widely used on lower sections of the house and to buttress the south-facing terraces, helping to anchor the house to the site. Timber siding (western red cedar) is also in evidence, along with zinc cladding, while integrated planters filled with grasses help soften the outline of the house.

'The zinc has a dark, earthy quality,' explains Radziner. 'To me it looks like the bark of a tree – even the pine trees in the shadows have that kind of blackness. It helps the house recede and blend with the environment. Using greenery like the grasses around the entrance and other parts of the house helps to knit the house together with the surrounding landscape. Wherever we can, we always try and do that.'

A sequence of terraces includes an outdoor dining area and a lounge arranged around a stone-bordered fire pit. From here, there is access to the main living areas of the house through sliding glass doors. Inside, stone walls and cedar ceilings lend a rustic–modern character, while contrasting with the polished concrete floors. The floor plan allows for easy connections between the interlinked spaces, but individual zones have a clear identity of their own. The living room is partially separated from the dining area by a double-sided stone fireplace, and the dining area, set within a central, double-height atrium that also includes the staircase, is partly separated from the kitchen by the arrangement of the counters and a breakfast bar. Yet there is still an impression of openness, with light circulating freely, bringing out the tones and textures of the materials.

The layout and the fluid relationship between inside and out allows for a great deal of flexibility as to how the house is used, according to the needs of the family and the changing seasons. The same principle continues upstairs, where there is a pair of bunk rooms for the children and their friends, plus two guest suites, while the owners retain a sense of quiet seclusion in the master suite contained in the satellite. Here, too, they have some of the best views in the house, looking out across the towering pines and the mountains beyond.

The house features a strong relationship between inside and out, with balconies forming outdoor living spaces. The terrace alongside the sitting room includes a fire pit.

SITE PLAN

The dining room and sitting room are partially separated by the fireplace. The dining table is a custom-made piece, while the dining chairs are from Viesso. In the sitting room, the sofa by the window is an Edward Wormley design; the patterned settee, coffee tables and lounge chairs are all custom made.

The use of stone and timber for the interiors helps tie the house to the rural site. The cabinet in the hallway is a Brazilian piece from the Thomas Hayes Gallery in Los Angeles; the painting in the sitting room is by Julian Opie.

The master suite sits within a smaller satellite
building alongside the main house, and enjoys
some of the best views. The bedroom features a
custom-designed bed, headboard and nightstands
by the architects and a reading light by Leonardo
Marelli, plus a vintage nickel-plated lamp.

MAISON BISCUIT

Lyon, France
Architectes Urbanistes Pierre Minassian

The house that architect Pierre Minassian built for himself and his family sits on a steeply sloping hillside at the edge of a small village, not far from Lyon in the Rhône-Alpes region of France. Gently pushed into the rugged terrain, the two-storey house looks downwards into valley pasture and across the landscape to woodland and hills. Horses graze in the pasture, even in the winter months, and the view is calming, restorative and engaging.

Maison Biscuit takes its name from a series of lozenges, wired together into a lattice curtain, which forms a brise soleil at the front of the house on the upper level. Originally these 'biscuits' were made of timber by Minassian himself, but have since been replaced by more durable aluminium lozenges. They provide a welcome degree of shade to the bedrooms and bathrooms on the upper level of the building, which faces eastwards across the open countryside, while the shadows and patterns that they create inside the house carry echoes of Arabian *mashrabiya* screens.

The main entrance of the house is also on the upper level, to the rear, where the building meets the back garden, the driveway and the street beyond. A glass doorway and vast windows around it bring natural light into the upper storey, while also creating a degree of transparency at the centre of the house, where a double-height atrium offers a key focal point around which the circulation and floor plan are arranged. A glass balcony at the upper entry hallway and landing looks down into this atrium, while a floating steel staircase invites visitors downwards to the main living spaces.

The open-plan living area of the house is arranged around the atrium, which is crowned by a dramatic Flos chandelier. This long, fluid universal space opens up to dramatic views out across the landscape, as well as a terrace alongside the house. A seating zone is arranged at one end and the kitchen and dining area at the other. But the lower storey is not entirely open plan. Minassian sought to create a balance here between shared space and creating a number of more intimate rooms for himself, his wife Estelle, an English-language teacher, and their two daughters. At one end of the house is a family lounge that also serves

The house looks down into a gentle valley and across to rolling hills and woodland; a swimming pool is positioned just below the main building. The brise soleil on the upper level is composed of a lattice of interlinked ceramic 'biscuits'.

as a television room. A semi-partitioned library sits beyond a fireplace at the other end of the house, as does a generously proportioned studio space behind closed doors, mostly used by Minassian as a music room; guitars and piano are a particular favourite with the family.

'I wanted to have a house with easy communication between all the main spaces, but also a sense of intimacy,' says Minassian, who has his own architectural practice based in Lyon, and works on a mixture of residential and cultural projects. 'The family didn't want me playing the guitar in the living room, and I didn't want the television in here either. So that was the challenge. And at the same time we wanted the sensation of being in a big house, with plenty of space around us.'

The furniture is a mix of a number of bespoke pieces designed by the architect, including the coffee table and dining table, with mid-century classics by Eero Saarinen and Charles and Ray Eames. The two paintings in the living room are also by Minassian, and sit against a simple backdrop of crisp, white walls, polished concrete floors and custom elements such as the steel stairs and fireplace. Warmth is lent by splashes of colour throughout the interiors, as well as the biscuit brise soleil, ever-present across the upper storey, and particularly by the landscape itself, which is green and verdant in summer, although rather different in character when the snow falls and the trees and pasture are dusted in white. The house has an escapist quality, which Minassian embraces.

'I love being an architect, but it does create a lot of daily challenges,' he says. 'So I like to come back home and escape into music and into the house itself. It's a very good place to come back to. I come down the stairs, see the big view and I feel better.'

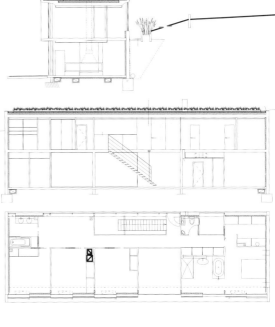

The house is pushed into the hillside, with the entrance on the upper level to the rear. Bedrooms are also positioned on the upper storey, with the main living spaces together with a music studio on the lower floor.

FLOOR PLANS

The main living area is an open-plan space
on the lower storey, with a seating area within
a double-height space at the centre and a
dining area and kitchen to one side. The sofa is
from Indera, while the two rocking chairs are
Charles and Ray Eames designs from Vitra.

The kitchen and dining area feature a bespoke dining table designed by the architect, with Eero Saarinen dining chairs from Knoll. The master bedroom upstairs features an open-plan bathroom and tub, while the biscuit brise soleil provides both shading and privacy.

OUTPOST

Bellevue, Idaho, USA
Olson Kundig Architects

Idaho is a state of extremes. Rugged, wild and beautiful, this is America in the raw. The summers are hot here, but the winters in this landscape of mountains and desert can be dramatic, with plenty of snow and temperatures that fall well below freezing. This is where Jan MacFarland Cox has made her home, known as the Outpost, which opens up to the rolling countryside of Blaine County, in the southern part of the state.

'I love the winter here,' says Cox. 'The snow is several feet deep for four months or more, and the landscape becomes very sculptural, with the amazing sun and changing light. We are in the widest part of a valley, where the mountains and high desert meet and the views are 360 degrees. The foothills form a natural bowl around us, and there are glimpses of the snow-covered peaks to the north.'

Sitting within this epic countryside, the house itself stands like a piece of sculpture: a flat-roofed, rectangular form, punctured by vast panels of glass that open out to the landscape, complemented by a walled garden, where fruit trees, roses and wisteria are protected from the elements. The building was essentially designed around one open, elevated and multifunctional room, overlooked by a mezzanine bedroom, but with a separate studio/office, as well as utility spaces on a lower entry level.

'The combined studio and home aspect was always crucial,' says Cox, an artist and designer who works in a wide range of mediums, from photography to metalwork to ice. 'The original design was much larger than the one we ended up with, but the connected house and walled garden were always a given. The garden was a natural progression of the house, and was for practical, as well as aesthetic reasons.'

Cox has known the area for many years. Her father was a peripatetic architect, who brought his family to the region several times during Cox's childhood, taking advantage of the ski season. For a number of years she split her time between Idaho and the San Francisco Bay Area, but moved back to the nearby town of Ketchum around twenty-three years ago. It was her late father

The house and its walled garden are reminiscent of a compound farmstead or ranch; the garden walls help protect planting from extreme weather.

who actually bought the plot of land where Cox's house now stands, intending to build a solar house, which never happened. Years later, it fell to his daughter to create a striking home within this mesmerizing tract of countryside.

Cox first began considering building a home here around fifteen years ago, thinking she might design the house herself, but was struck by the work of architect Tom Kundig of the Seattle-based practice Olson Kundig. Many of Kundig's houses are thoughtful and highly imaginative responses to rural landscapes, sitting in the countryside like pieces of land art. It was just this level of artistry and character that drew Cox to his work.

'I saw Tom's work in a magazine and I contacted him,' she says. 'We had a great connection in approach and philosophy, and as he had also grown up skiing in this area the project spoke to him immediately. I hadn't been "shopping" for an architect, so working with somebody so talented yet down to earth was a gift.'

Kundig adds: 'The landscape is really the soul of the house. Every decision made about the building was relative to the background of that big, powerful and subtle landscape. So for an architect that grew up in a similar landscape, this commission reached into the soul of my childhood memories, and perhaps my most important memories: the big sky, the rolling hills, the smell of the dry grasses and sage, the crunch of the wind-blown snow.'

The warm interiors contrast with the cool, sculpted form of the outside of the house, which was finally completed in 2007. Architect and client made use of recycled fir for floorboards and some interior finishes; steel bookshelves, backed with storage compartments, help form a balcony to protect the mezzanine-level bedroom. Cox inherited a number of pieces of furniture for the house, while others have been collected over the years. Some of these were adapted, such as the round, maple-topped table, which came out west with her pioneer ancestors in covered wagons in the mid-nineteenth century; the new base is her own design. Other items, such as the bronze and steel desk in her studio, were designed by Cox from scratch, within a creative collaboration that has produced a unique home of very individual character.

The outline of the house is crisp and sculptural, with large and dramatic window openings carefully placed to filter light and allow for a strong sense of connection with the surrounding mountains.

The main living areas are contained within one elevated multifunctional space that makes the most of the wide-open views; the master bedroom is contained within a mezzanine, while a studio and utility spaces are positioned on the lower level of the building.

HAUS AM WEINBERG

Stuttgart, Germany
UNStudio

Positioned on a sloping hillside site, bordered with trees, the Haus am Weinberg has a fascinating dual aspect. To one side lie the suburbs of the city of Stuttgart, but to the other is a collection of vineyards, emblematic of a proud wine-making history in the region, with the main varieties including Lemberger, Trollinger, Spätburgunder, Riesling, Silvaner and Kerner. The vineyards and the landscape were a key source of inspiration for the design of the house, which features a vaulted wine cellar and tasting room positioned almost at the very heart of the building.

'I was fascinated by the landscape here and the way that you could walk between certain parts of it and the vineyards,' says architect Ben van Berkel of UNStudio. 'The whole idea of transporting that experience into the house was the key. I talked about a parallax experience, which is echoed back into the house. When you enter the house, you walk up the stairs and look out, and it's a similar experience to that of walking through the vineyards.'

The house, commissioned by a family with a passion for architecture and design, also explores ideas of dynamic movement and spatial complexity seen in a number of the firm's buildings. This fluid dynamism is encapsulated in the idea of the 'twist', which features in several landmark projects, including the Mercedes-Benz Museum in Stuttgart. Here, the twist is partially expressed through the design of the sculptural staircase, which forms a focal point for the building, but also helps to organize the circulation and volumes of the house as it winds its way through the structure.

'The staircase does a lot of things,' says Van Berkel. 'It helps stabilize the structure of the house, but it is also a central meeting point, where the members of the household come together. As you move up and down the staircase you orient yourself within the house. So it's not only a structural, but also a social moment in the house – just as there's the metaphorical notion of the twist, there is also a literal, constructive physical twist as well.'

Upon entering the house, which is pushed into the slope of the hillside, the staircase is the dominant element on the ground floor. This is the subservient

The house sits on a sloping hillside alongside the vineyards for which the region is well-known. This rugged landscape and the vineyards themselves were key factors in the design of the building.

level of the home, given over to guest accommodation, utility spaces and the wine cellar and tasting room. The house reveals its true character on the level above, which cradles the main living spaces, the kitchen and a double-height dining area that looks out onto a generous terrace to the rear of the building and upwards to the vineyards. The dining table, then, assumes particular importance within one of the grandest and most open parts of the home.

Dual sitting rooms, placed alongside one another, establish an intriguing sense of contrast between the two spaces. One is open and light, with large windows and warm oak floors. The other is enclosed, with black-panelled walls and ceilings; this is an evening lounge and music room with the atmosphere of a sophisticated, contemporary private members' club or library, designed with a very individual personality. The upper storey of the house is largely devoted to the master suite, as well as a library within a mezzanine gallery that overlooks the dining area below.

Many bespoke features, including the main fireplace, kitchen and master bathroom, layer the house, which has been carefully tailored to the needs of the clients, as well as the particular requirements of the site and context. The notion of a highly tailored solution continues outside into the landscaping and terraces around the building, which include a water pool near the entrance and a custom dining area and outdoor kitchen. The terrace itself forms an outdoor room, looking up to the vineyards and the hills. It is part of the constant but varied relationship between the house and the landscape beyond.

'The landscape and the light changes over the course of the year, so the number of experiences keeps growing and creates new surprises,' says Van Berkel. 'Whenever I am there with the clients, they tell me they can't believe that even after a few years of living in the house every day, they discover something new.'

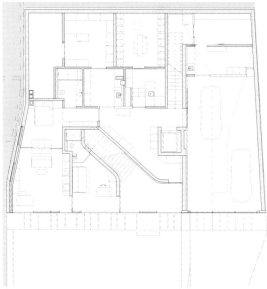

FLOOR PLAN

Most of the principal living spaces are at mid-level. The double-height dining area is a particular focal point, with vast windows at this corner of the house framing a select view of the vineyards.

From inside the house, the scale of the dining area and the importance of the hillside views becomes clear; an adjoining terrace serves as an outdoor dining room in the summer.

The sculpted staircase is the focal point of the whole house, helping to organize the key spaces and providing a central meeting point around which daily life revolves.

Dual sitting rooms at mid-level offer a
powerful contrast between light and dark,
openness and enclosure, with one space
more suited to daytime living and the
other an atmospheric evening retreat.

DIRECTORY

**ARCHITECTES URBANISTES
PIERRE MINASSIAN**
Maison Biscuit, pp. 228–35
4, place Rouville, 69001 Lyon, France
aum.fr

ATELIER KASTELIC BUFFEY
Maison Glissade, pp. 86–93
25a Morrow Avenue, Suite 202,
Toronto, Ontario M6R 2H9, Canada
akb.ca

ANTONIE BERTHERAT-KIOES
Usine Gruben, pp. 146–57
Avenue Rosemont 10,
1208 Geneva, Switzerland

ALBERTO CAMPO BAEZA
Olnick Spanu House, pp. 208–17
Almirante 4, 5º b,
28004 Madrid, Spain
campobaeza.com

CHEVALLIER ARCHITECTES
Piolet, pp. 138–45
225, rue Paccard,
74400 Chamonix, France
chevallier-architectes.fr

**DIETRICH UNTERTRIFALLER
ARCHITEKTEN**
Strolz House, pp. 94–103
Arlbergstraße 117,
6900 Bregenz, Austria
Flachgasse 35–37,
1150 Vienna, Austria
Höhenweg 33,
9000 St Gallen, Switzerland
dietrich.untertrifaller.com

DUALCHAS ARCHITECTS
Colbost House, pp. 60–7
Duisdale Beag, Sleat,
Isle of Skye IV43 8QU, UK
Unit 4, Building 5,
62 Templeton Street,
Glasgow G40 1DA, UK
dualchas.com

NOÉ DUCHAUFOUR-LAWRANCE
Chalet La Transhumance, pp. 128–37
8, passage de la Bonne Graine,
75011 Paris, France
noeduchaufourlawrance.com

DUST
Tucson Mountain Retreat, pp. 68–73
dustdb.com

HHF ARCHITECTS
Tsai Residence, pp. 172–81
Allschwilerstraße 71a,
4055 Basel, Switzerland
hhf.ch

JAMES HOUSTON
Timber Lake House, pp. 50–9
houstonphoto.com

HURST SONG ARCHITEKTEN
Holzkristal, pp. 32–41
Badenerstraße 156,
8004 Zurich, Switzerland
hurstsong.ch

INCORPORATED
Sixteen Doors House, pp. 14–21
9 East 19th Street, Floor 9,
New York, New York 10003, USA
incorporatedny.com

To Danielle, for her love and support

The authors would like to express their particular thanks and
gratitude to all of the architects and designers who have helped to
make this book possible and to the many mountain homeowners who
assisted us and showed us such generous hospitality on our travels.

We would also like to thank the following: Faith Bradbury; Tanya
Buchanan; Chalet Châtelet; Stephanie Fischer, Nira Alpina; Daniela
and Philippe Frutiger, Giardino Hotel Group; Katja Grauwiler;
Danielle Miller; Richard Pike; Gerold and Katia Schneider, Hotel
Almhof Schneider; Neale Whitaker; Vera Wichmann, Hotel Therme
Vals; and Gordon Wise.

Thanks are also due to all at Thames & Hudson for their support
and encouragement, particularly Lucas Dietrich, Elain McAlpine and
Adélia Sabatini, and to Anna Perotti.

All plans and drawings supplied by the architects. All photographs by
Richard Powers, apart from the following: *60–7* Andrew Lee; *68–73*
© Jeff Goldberg/Esto; *244–9* Christian Richters; 236–43 Tim Bies/
Olson Kundig Architects; *250–3* Iwan Baan

On the cover: *Villa Vals, Switzerland, by SeARCH*

First published in the United Kingdom in 2014
by Thames & Hudson Ltd,
181A High Holborn, London WC1V 7QX

First paperback edition 2016

Mountain Modern © 2014 Thames & Hudson Ltd,
London
Text © 2014 Dominic Bradbury
Photographs © 2014 Richard Powers

Designed by Anna Perotti

British Library Cataloguing-in-Publication Data
A catalogue record for this book is available from
the British Library

ISBN 978-0-500-29256-3

Printed and bound in China by Everbest Printing Co Ltd

To find out about all our publications, please visit
www.thamesandhudson.com.
There you can subscribe to our e-newsletter, browse
or download our current catalogue, and buy any titles
that are in print.